AF484926

from student to teacher

A JOURNEY OF TRANSFORMATION AND MANIFESTATION

T.L. WORKMAN

Copyright © 2024 T.L. Workman

All rights reserved. No part of this book may be reproduced, stored in a retrieval system, or transmitted in any form or by any means (mechanical, photographic, electronic, recording, or otherwise) without the author's prior written permission, except for brief quotations embodied in articles and reviews.

The author of this book is not a medical professional and does not provide medical advice. The content of this book is intended for informational purposes only and should not be considered a substitute for professional medical advice, diagnosis, or treatment. It is recommended to consult with a qualified healthcare provider before deciding or taking any actions based on the information provided in this book. The author and the publisher disclaim any liability or responsibility for any loss or damage incurred as a direct or indirect result of using or applying any information in this book.

Designed by T.L. Workman
Trade Paper ISBN: 979-8-3304-3430-5
First Published on June 1, 2024
Printed in the United States of America

To my beloved Kiana,

I hope that the wisdom shared within these pages
ignites a radiant spark within you —
a spark that emboldens you to live a life without boundaries,
fearlessly embarking on the extraordinary
journey towards your dreams.
Know that I wholeheartedly believe in you, kid.

Mary,

Wherever you are ... thank you.

CONTENTS

> *"When the student is ready,*
> *the teacher will appear."*
>
> UNKNOWN

INTRODUCTION

MY STORY

A TEMPEST OF nature raged with unbridled fury in the heart of the New Mexican desert. Hailstones pelted relentlessly while lightning bolts streaked across the darkened sky, illuminating the vast expanse with ethereal brilliance. Thunder roared like a battle cry, shaking the very ground beneath the wheels of my car. It was an afternoon unlike any other, a scene that seemed plucked from the pages of J.R.R. Tolkien's epic tale, *The Hobbit*.

As the torrential downpour raged, my wiper blades struggled, unable to match the relentless assault of rain. I grappled with the blurred landscape, uncertain if the rain or my teardrops obscured my view. Semis whizzed past, perilously close to my car, their presence a stark reminder of the treacherous mountain pass that loomed ahead, ready to plunge me into oblivion.

Overwhelmed by fear, I sought sanctuary on the roadside. This storm reflected my life, I thought ironically. It was a complete and utter mess. I wiped my eyes and blew my nose, unable to stop the uncontrollable sobs that were beginning to rock my body.

My life was undergoing significant changes and upheaval. To create a better environment for our family, my fiancé and I moved from Murrieta, California, to his hometown of Cincinnati, Ohio. We purchased a home, invested time and effort in its renovation, and secured new jobs. Everything seemed perfect.

Until it wasn't.

Amidst the chaos of packing our old home, the once-promising relationship brimming with hope and possibilities had crumbled, leaving me at a crucial turning point.

With goodbyes said and necessary closures made, I stood at a crossroads, contemplating two paths. I could either stay in a familiar place where I felt safe and had family or take the leap and move to Ohio, where I had a job waiting to support me.

Regardless of which option I chose, one thing was sure: both meant a fresh start. The thought of moving alone to a new state, with no familiar faces or support system, filled me with anxiety and doubt. It was a daunting and terrifying risk, yet it beckoned me to be brave.

And so, here I was, en route to Ohio. If ever there was an act of blind faith, this was it—or stupidity. The journey had been uneventful until this point. Then, out of nowhere, the heavens unleashed their wrath upon me. What determination I had faltered. Was this a bad omen for the road ahead? Were the heavens telling me to turn back?

I often seek guidance from my father at pivotal moments. Thinking of my father instantly transports me to Heisler Park in Laguna Beach, overlooking the tide pools. That day, the rocks were glistening under the fading rain. We were taking our early evening walk, as we usually do. I was lost in teenage reverie when my father came beside me and hugged me.

"Look," he said, pointing to the sky. "It's a double rainbow."

I looked up, shocked to behold such a beautiful sight against the backdrop of the ocean and approaching dusk. The double rainbow stretched across the sky in brilliant colors like a bridge of hope. It was my first time witnessing such a phenomenon, and I struggled to grasp such breathtaking beauty.

My father hugged me tighter. "I love you," he said.

You could have struck me in the face then, and I wouldn't have flinched. My father, who rarely showed affection or emotion to me, had rendered me motionless. Upon hearing his words, my inner child, who yearned for love and affection, exploded into happiness and joy.

"I love you too, Dad," I hugged him back, choking back tears. That moment, etched in my memory, remains my happiest with him.

But Dad was long gone. He had passed away unexpectedly due to a brain aneurysm nearly four years prior. Although he was no longer physically present, not much else had changed. I still found myself seeking his guidance at times, and this was one of them.

"Dad, please give me a sign I'm going in the right direction," I whispered, staring into the darkness ahead as sadness enveloped me like a dark shroud.

Seconds later, I reached the peak of the mountain pass and started my descent. Above me, storm clouds loomed ominously while lightning bolts streaked across the sky with an air of wrath and vengeance. The resounding thunder roars seemed to carry a warning from the heavens, urging me to reconsider my path. In the distance, I could see relentless sheets of rain cascading down, extending as far as the eye could see. If ever there was a sign, it was unmistakable and impossible to ignore.

But amid nature's furious onslaught, a glimmer of hope emerged. Below, nestled in the valley, there lay a sanctuary untouched by the storm's wrath. It was as if the tempest itself recoiled in fear, encircling the valley but unable to breach its boundaries. No clouds threatened overhead; only the radiant rays of the afternoon sun pierced through the atmosphere. And there, within that refuge, stretched across the sky like a magnificent and glorious bridge of hope, appeared a pair of rainbows.

Hi, Dad.

At that moment, what little self-composure I had vanished. I crumpled as tears poured from within me as if I had bottled them up for years. With a mixture of nervousness but renewed determination, I steeled myself to embrace the unknown.

I gripped the steering wheel tighter and drove.

HOW I DISCOVERED THE LAW OF ATTRACTION

"When the student is ready, the teacher will appear." This phrase expresses a timeless wisdom that has consistently comforted me throughout my journey, especially at crucial moments. It's a gentle reminder that the Universe has a way of guiding us, bringing the right teachings and lessons when we are truly prepared to receive them.

I settled into Ohio quietly, working as the marketing director for a production homebuilder. The job gave me creative freedom to show off my talents and proved incredibly challenging yet rewarding. To outsiders, I was smiling and happy. But inside, I was dying. The complete uprooting of my previous life and the pain and loss from the end of my relationship led me to question not only myself but the overall trajectory of my existence.

Unhealed wounds, past traumas, and fragmented aspects of my identity surged to the surface as if suddenly unleashed. I stood at the precipice of my deepest desires, fears, and unresolved issues, unleashing intense emotions. I had never felt so adrift in my life.

I carried the heavy burden of my anguish while time continued its relentless march, guiding me through the intricate stages of grief. During this vulnerable phase, I sought solace in solitude and nature, yearning for healing, clarity, and a sense of purpose. Like a chrysalis, I withdrew inward, fully aware that a profound transformation was unfolding, yet uncertain of what it would ultimately yield.

One afternoon, my boss assigned me to visit our company's off-site design center to meet with the design consultant. This visit aimed to understand their methods so I could create accurate marketing materials depicting their process.

While driving, I lost myself in deep thoughts about the meaning of life. As I often do in the car, I vocalized my contemplations, questioning whether there was a higher purpose beyond survival and suffering.

"What was I made for?"

Instantly, that familiar phrase teasingly echoed deeply within the recesses of my mind: "When the student is ready, the teacher will appear."

"I'm ready!" I cried, my voice cracking with the weight of months spent mired in grief and stagnancy. "Show me!"

When I arrived at the design center, a woman named Mary, whom I had never met, greeted me. Mary, a radiant blonde in her late thirties, had worked part-time as a design consultant with the company for six months while pursuing vocational studies. Despite my usual difficulty connecting with strangers, Mary exuded a genuine, undeniable warmth and authenticity. Our conversation quickly moved beyond work-related matters, delving into discussions about family, children, and general well-being. Unexpectedly, Mary turned her head to the side, intently studying me, and asked, "Are you alright?"

Mary's gaze bore a weight that left no doubt in my mind—she already knew the answer to her question. It was as if she could see beyond the facade of my smile. I hesitated, unsure how much to reveal. Yet, compelled by an inexplicable force, I found myself opening to her, sharing every intricate detail, even as a part of me braced for the possibility of being deemed insane.

To my astonishment, Mary embraced the complexities of my journey without a trace of judgment. She accepted the rawness of my experiences and the uncertainties that plagued my mind. A newfound sense of acceptance and understanding enfolded me in her presence, dispelling any fear of being misunderstood.

It was then that Mary revealed her path. She disclosed she was attending vocational school in Florida, pursuing certification as a Reiki practitioner. With earnest enthusiasm, Mary explained the transformative power of Reiki—an ancient healing practice centered on channeling universal life force energy to nurture physical, emotional, and spiritual well-being. Sensing the imbalances within my energy field, she humbly offered her insights, feeling compelled to help me.

She revealed that my experiences and life changes had triggered a spiritual awakening within me, a concept I had never encountered before. This awakening brought about profound shifts and challenges that shook the very foundations of my existence. Mary stressed the significance of breaking free from familiar patterns and routines, which would allow new insights, perspectives, and possibilities to emerge.

As I navigate this uncharted territory, I will feel compelled to explore the depths of my essence in search of meaning, connection, and a deeper understanding of myself and the world around me. In this fertile ground of transformation, the seeds of spiritual awakening will take root, inviting me to embrace my true nature, embody my divine essence, and seek self-discovery and inner transformation.

Intrigued, I couldn't help but feel a shiver run up my spine as I uttered the familiar request, "I'm ready. Show me." Modestly, Mary clarified she had yet to attain certification as a practitioner herself. She assured me she could steer me in the right direction. She mentioned the abundance of skilled practitioners in Florida, where she pursued her studies, and suggested that I explore local and online avenues. Our conversation stretched for hours, seamlessly shifting between the intricacies of our company's processes and discussions on personal growth. We spoke and laughed like long-lost friends, effortlessly picking up where we had left off.

As our time ended, I felt a strong sense of synchronicity, as if the Universe had heard my pleas and arranged our meeting. I departed with a newfound sense of direction after months of stagnation.

Until that point in my life, spirituality, belief, and religion had resided on the outskirts of my mind. I had viewed the world through the lens of practicality and skepticism, considering myself a rational thinker. I dismissed it as nonexistent if I couldn't perceive something with my senses or explain it through scientific reasoning. But that night, I willingly allowed myself to venture into the mysterious and unknown, determined to heal my brokenness.

Engrossed in my research, I dipped into energy healing modalities, meditation practices, and breathwork techniques. With every article I read, it was as if a missing puzzle piece found its rightful place. Before the night ended, I took the initiative to contact a spiritual teacher in Florida, filled with enthusiasm to learn about energy work and meditation.

A rare sense of tranquility washed over me as I closed my eyes that night. It provided a temporary respite from the perpetual restlessness that had consumed me for what felt like an eternity. Embracing the possibilities, I drifted off to sleep, grateful for Mary and that serendipitous encounter.

The following day, I thanked my boss for arranging the meeting with Mary. However, his confusion was evident when I mentioned her name. He clarified that the design consultant's name was Maura, not

Mary. It suddenly dawned on me I must have misheard her during our initial introduction. Nevertheless, this realization didn't dampen my happiness about meeting her. I shrugged it off and continued with my responsibilities.

A week later, I would get another chance to see Maura when she visited our office for a meeting. I was thrilled to have the opportunity to express my gratitude and update her on my progress. At that point, I had enrolled in a series of one-on-one meditation sessions and had already completed one. I could feel the improvements in my well-being.

I was engrossed in my work, back turned to the door, when I overheard the receptionist say, "Hi, Maura." I turned around with a smile, ready to say hello, but to my astonishment, the woman standing in the doorway bore no resemblance to the woman I had encountered. This revelation perplexed me—were two women of the same unique names working in the same department? Instantly, I knew I had not misheard the name. It was Mary.

Determined to uncover the truth, I approached Maura to say hello. She was an older woman with blond hair, petite, and seemingly untouched by the passage of time. Her warm smile instantly drew me in. Eager to unravel the enigma, I recounted my meeting with Mary, hoping Maura could shed some light on the situation.

Maura clarified that she and her part-time assistant worked only at the design center, and her assistant did not match the description of the woman I had encountered. Furthermore, her assistant had been absent on the day of the encounter, adding to the mystery. Since Maura herself had been out of the office, we were both perplexed about who had a key and had been waiting for me.

Despite my efforts to investigate and gather information, the discrepancy surrounding Mary's identity and presence persisted. It seemed as if she had appeared and vanished. I contacted anyone she might work with, but no one knew her. The mystery surrounding Mary's existence deepened, leaving me with more questions than answers.

Amidst Mary's identity uncertainty, her guidance was what I needed. What had started as a mere curiosity swiftly awoke a sleeping giant fueled by a potent blend of intuition and determination. I dove headfirst into the depths of discovery with open arms.

I eagerly embraced the role of a student, immersing myself in the wisdom of energy practitioners, gurus, healers, monks, and shamans. My studies encompassed diverse meditation practices and techniques, cultivating mindfulness, clarity, and inner peace. These transformative sessions allowed me to observe my thoughts and emotions without judgment, forging a profound connection with my inner self.

Driven by an insatiable desire for personal growth, I explored healing modalities, delving into Reiki, chakra balancing, and the subtle body. The knowledge gained opened new dimensions of understanding and possibility. Through breathwork practices and Emotional Freedom Techniques (EFT), I released emotional blockages and anxiety, triggering profound healing and self-exploration.

Throughout this transformative journey, I avidly absorbed knowledge like a sponge. It was a constant exploration, uncovering truths and unlocking the boundless potential within. Over time, my understanding and appreciation of spirituality expanded. I realized that there is a vast realm of knowledge, wisdom, and interconnectedness beyond what can be explained by science and the rational mind. I recognized that certain aspects of the human experience transcend logic and that accessing them requires intuition, inner exploration, and connection with the greater whole.

Through these practices and teachings, I healed and integrated the broken parts of myself. I gained a deeper understanding of my experiences, their lessons, and the patterns I unconsciously perpetuated, which empowered me to move forward with renewed purpose and authenticity.

I can't help but laugh a little as I contemplate the irony. While others sought spiritual enlightenment in temples, ashrams, and sacred sites, my grand quest for cosmic wisdom led me to ... *Ohio.*

I stumbled upon manifestation and the Law of Attraction during this transformative period. Though I had heard it mentioned countless times, I had yet to pay genuine attention. *Thoughts, emotions, and feelings as energy and vibrations?* The old version of me would call this nonsense, dismissing it as mere woo-woo. But new me? The new me told myself to embrace it.

Much like my previous pursuits, I immersed myself in extensive research, devouring every piece of literature and media available. Guided by my analytical mind, which craved an understanding of the mechanics and inner workings, I didn't simply accept its promise at face value.

Like a mad scientist conducting meticulous experiments, I kept journals in which I methodically dissected and analyzed its components to gain understanding. Each experiment acted as a stepping stone, leading me toward unraveling the mysteries and intricacies of manifestation. Through trial and error, I refined my approach and fine-tuned my understanding.

To my astonishment, the floodgates of the Universe swung wide open. As I began applying the teachings, I witnessed the miraculous unfolding of my most profound dreams and desires. It was as if a switch had been flipped after a lifetime of dormancy, igniting a sense of purpose that reverberated through every fiber of my being. I had stumbled upon a treasure trove and felt an overwhelming compulsion to shout and share it with the world.

In that critical moment, I felt an undeniable and authentic calling that possessed a power so immense it seemed capable of breaking the sound barrier and rousing dormant galaxies from their slumber. The clarity I experienced was absolute.

This is what I was made for.

WHY I WROTE THIS BOOK

Exploring the profound influence of distinguished teachers throughout history is essential to shed light on the creation of this book. Gautama Buddha, also known as Siddhartha Gautama, emerged as a visionary spiritual guide and the founder of Buddhism. Born into royalty in ancient India, Siddhartha initially led a luxurious life but became disillusioned with worldly pursuits. He embarked on a quest for enlightenment and achieved it beneath a bodhi tree, becoming the Buddha. The rest of his life was dedicated to imparting the principles of Buddhism, emphasizing wisdom, ethical conduct, and liberation from suffering encapsulated in the *Four Noble Truths* and the *Noble Eightfold Path*.

Sir Isaac Newton, a renowned English physicist, mathematician, and astronomer, holds an indelible place in scientific achievement. As a student at the University of Cambridge, Newton immersed himself in the study of mathematics and physics. His groundbreaking discoveries, including the laws of motion and the universal law of gravitation, revolutionized our understanding of the physical world. Newton's work laid the foundation of classical mechanics, leaving a lasting impact on physics and astronomy. Later in his career, Newton assumed the role of a professor at Cambridge, sharing his knowledge and insights with students.

Mahatma Gandhi transcended his academic background to become a teacher in life itself. His teachings and philosophy of nonviolent resistance, known as *satyagraha*, were pivotal in guiding India's struggle for independence from British colonial rule. Despite his professional background as a lawyer, Gandhi advocated for the powerful principles of truth, nonviolence, and civil disobedience as catalysts for social and political change. Gandhi emerged as a venerable instructor through his writings, speeches, and actions, imparting invaluable life lessons while championing the causes of justice, equality, and purposeful existence.

These historical exemplars vividly illustrate how individuals from diverse domains, spanning spirituality, science, and life, can emerge as transformative teachers, leaving an enduring imprint on the world and shaping history.

Deep within every individual resides an innate yearning for growth and progress, an insatiable hunger to flourish in all dimensions of life. This profound longing encompasses the vast expanse of our existence, encompassing realms such as career, relationships, well-being, abundance, creativity, and spirituality. My genuine intention and mission is to witness the magnificent unfolding of your limitless inner potential, see you transcend the burdens of suffering, and behold the extraordinary capabilities that lie dormant within you.

This book offers a thoughtfully curated collection of my accumulated timeless teachings and wisdom. By sharing these insights, I aim to provide the tools and techniques necessary for you to rewrite your script, transform your destiny, and manifest a reality once confined to the realm of dreams. As you delve into this wisdom, you will gradually uncover the profound influence your thoughts, beliefs, and emotions have on shaping your reality. I sincerely wish this discovery ignites a spark within you, as it did within me, compelling you to share these teachings with the world and embrace your role as a teacher, empowering others to reach their greatest self.

While attaining the stature of Buddha, Newton, or Gandhi may appear unattainable, each of us has the potential to impact the world. Just as a tiny snowball can trigger an avalanche, our behavior, the sharing of knowledge, effective communication, emotional influence, living our values, and the ripple effect of our actions can inspire positive change in the lives of others. In turn, this contributes to our communities' overall growth and well-being.

As you progress through these chapters, you may feel like déjà vu and notice a pattern of repetition. This intentional repetition serves a purpose akin to a Jedi mind trick. It reprograms your mind, tapping into the walls of your subconscious, reinforcing new beliefs and thought patterns, and allowing them to sink deeper into your consciousness. Trust that this repetition is intentional and designed to facilitate your transformation.

I implore you to approach this with an open heart and curious mind. Allow the wisdom within these pages to guide, empower, and inspire you to make positive changes in your life. Be receptive to the insights that resonate most deeply, for they hold the keys to unlocking your fullest potential.

That pivotal encounter with Mary from years ago remains etched deep within my memory, intricately woven with purpose and significance. It is a perpetual reminder of the extraordinary possibilities that await us when we follow our intuition and embrace the unknown's transformative power. I no longer seek to unravel the intricacies of that encounter. The specifics matter little, whether it was a chance meeting, a synchronistic event, or an encounter with a celestial messenger. What truly matters is its seismic impact on my personal and spiritual growth. It became the catalyst that shattered the confines of my old self, propelling me into a realm of limitless possibilities where transformation and evolution became unwavering companions.

PART I

the foundation

"*The cosmos is within us. We are made of star stuff.*
We are a way for the Universe to know itself."

CARL SAGAN

QUANTUM ENTANGLEMENT AND LAW OF ATTRACTION

THE BEGINNING

QUANTUM PHYSICS TAKES us on a captivating journey into the depths of our vast Universe, revealing a profound truth: everything around us, at its core, is composed of energy. As we venture into the subatomic realm, an astonishing revelation unfolds—a revelation that matter dissolves, leaving behind only pure energy. In this remarkable dissolution, the material world fades away, unveiling the underlying essence that permeates every facet of existence.

When we contemplate the early stages of our Universe, we encounter a primordial state teeming with a sea of minuscule particles intermingled with radiant light and boundless energy. This cosmic landscape starkly contrasts the familiar reality we perceive today. Over time, these tiny particles merged, forming bonds and forging connections. They engaged in an intricate dance so entwined that attempting to separate them became impossible. This interconnected web of energy is the very fabric of reality, forming the foundation of all that exists in our Universe.

Then came the awe-inspiring event known as the Big Bang—a monumental moment that catapulted our Universe into a phase of tremendous expansion, a cosmic unfolding that persists today. This expansion occurred at an inconceivable rate, stretching the fabric of space-time itself and giving rise to the fundamental forces and particles that would eventually coalesce into the structures of our cosmos. For 13.8+ billion years, this remarkable expansion gave birth to the formation of celestial bodies—stars, planets, and moons—creating the conditions necessary for life as we know it to emerge. And eventually, in the grand tapestry of cosmic evolution, it led to the extraordinary moment of your existence. It is a testament to the vastness and intricacy of the celestial symphony that you are here, a unique and precious expression of the Universe's unfolding story.

What is genuinely awe-inspiring is the realization that, at the molecular level, we are all composed of the same fundamental materials. We share a profound connection, an inherent oneness that transcends the boundaries of individuality. From the grandest galaxies to the tiniest atoms, we are all manifestations of the same energy source woven together in the intricate fabric of existence.

UNDERSTANDING QUANTUM ENTANGLEMENT

Quantum Entanglement is a captivating phenomenon that has expanded our understanding of the Universe. It challenges our classical notions of reality and reveals an interconnectedness that defies the limitations of space and time. Einstein often referred to this concept as "spooky action at a distance." This profound principle has been extensively studied and experimented upon in quantum mechanics, leading to groundbreaking discoveries about the true nature of our reality.

At its core, Quantum Entanglement reveals that if two objects are connected at a subatomic level and then separated by vast distances, when we interact with one of these objects, an instantaneous and corresponding action occurs with the other object, no matter how far apart they are. This remarkable behavior arises from the intertwined nature of particles at the quantum level, an interconnectedness that has existed since the very beginning of time itself.

To explore the nature of Quantum Entanglement, physicist John Bell proposed a series of experiments in the 1960s known as the Bell test experiments. The goal was to investigate whether particles possess predefined properties, called local hidden variables, which would explain their behavior without invoking entanglement. The experiments aimed at testing the boundaries of our current understanding and shed light on the nature of the quantum world.

Subsequent experiments, most notably those conducted by physicist Alain Aspect and his team in the 1980s, consistently violated Bell's inequalities. These experimental results provided compelling evidence for non-local correlations between entangled particles. In other words, the measurements of one particle's state instantaneously determined the state of its entangled partner, regardless of their spatial separation.

The groundbreaking findings from the Bell test experiments have firmly established the reality of Quantum Entanglement. They have shattered the notion of local realism, which posited the presence of underlying hidden variables that determined particles' behavior. Instead, these experiments have demonstrated that entangled particles share a unique interconnectedness that transcends our classical understanding of space and time.

This understanding invites us to embrace the undeniable truth of our interconnectedness and its profound implications. It serves as a gentle reminder we are not separate and isolated beings but integral parts of a vast and unified whole.

SEPARATION IS THE GREAT DELUSION, FOR AT THE
DEEPEST LEVEL, WE ARE ALL ENTANGLED -
PARTICLES, PLANETS, AND PEOPLE,
BOUND BY AN UNSEEN THREAD OF UNITY.

THE LAW OF ATTRACTION

The Law of Attraction is a powerful principle that highlights the significant role of our thoughts, emotions, and beliefs in shaping our reality. It suggests that the energetic vibrations we emit through our thoughts and feelings act as magnetic forces, drawing corresponding experiences into our lives. Simply put, we attract into our existence what we consistently focus on and align with vibrationally. This profound concept encourages us to be mindful of our internal state and to consciously direct our mental and emotional energy toward what we wish to manifest.

At the heart of the Law of Attraction are our thoughts. Our thoughts carry specific frequencies that resonate with similar frequencies in the Universe. This means maintaining positive and harmonious thoughts can attract positive outcomes and experiences. Conversely, negative thoughts can attract undesired circumstances, underscoring the importance of mindfully choosing our thoughts. This understanding offers hope and potential for positive change in our lives.

Emotions also play a vital role in the Law of Attraction. Emotions act as powerful energetic signals that amplify the vibrational frequency of our thoughts. When we align our thoughts with positive emotions such as joy, gratitude, and love, we enhance our ability to attract positive experiences. However, negative emotions like fear, doubt, and anger can hinder the manifestation process.

Additionally, our beliefs hold tremendous power under the Law of Attraction. Our core beliefs about ourselves, the world, and our ability to manifest shape our reality. Empowering beliefs facilitate manifestation while limiting beliefs can block it. We can significantly enhance our manifestation potential by cultivating beliefs aligned with our desired outcomes.

Understanding that the Law of Attraction operates with other universal principles and natural laws is essential. Myriad interconnected variables, including the choices and actions of others, societal structures, and natural processes, influence our reality. The Law of Attraction is not a magic wand that instantly transforms our lives but a tool for personal empowerment. It requires a holistic approach to integrating our beliefs, thoughts, emotions, and actions. This understanding helps us set realistic expectations and commit to conscious creation.

THE DANCE OF QUANTUM ENTANGLEMENT AND THE LAW OF ATTRACTION

The connection between Quantum Entanglement and the Law of Attraction lies in their shared recognition of the underlying interconnectedness of the Universe. Both concepts emphasize fundamental unity and interdependence, albeit from different perspectives.

Quantum Entanglement reveals that particles, once connected, remain inextricably linked regardless of the distance between them. This interconnectedness suggests that the separation we perceive in the physical world is illusory, and a more profound underlying unity exists. Similarly, the Law of Attraction acknowledges that our thoughts and emotions are not isolated events but energetic vibrations that interact with the larger energetic field of the Universe.

When we consider the dance of Quantum Entanglement and the

Law of Attraction together, a fascinating picture emerges. Our thoughts, emotions, and beliefs, which are energetic, can be seen as the entangled particles of our consciousness. Just as entangled particles instantaneously communicate and influence each other's states, our thoughts, and emotions instantaneously communicate and influence the energetic fabric of the Universe.

In this interconnected dance, our focused thoughts and positive emotions act as energetic magnets, attracting corresponding frequencies in the vast quantum field. Through this resonance, we attract and draw into our experiences, opportunities, and circumstances that align with our predominant vibrational state. We co-create our reality by entangling our consciousness with the entangled particles of the Universe.

EMBRACE THE INTERPLAY

The interplay between Quantum Entanglement and the Law of Attraction invites us to embrace our innate power as conscious creators, recognizing our profound connection to the Universe. By aligning our thoughts, emotions, and actions with our deepest desires and intentions, we can harness our potential to shape our reality and contribute to the unfolding story of the cosmos. As we travel this path of self-discovery, let us approach the intimate interplay between our inner world and the energetic tapestry of existence with reverence, wisdom, and a deep appreciation for the interconnectedness that binds us all.

"Whatever one frequently thinks and ponders upon, that will become the inclination of his mind."

GAUTAMA BUDDHA

CHAPTER 2

THE IMPACT OF THOUGHTS, EMOTIONS, AND BELIEFS

AN ETHEREAL MARVEL of nature emerges in the heart of eastern California, where the sun-kissed land meets the cerulean sky. It is Methuselah, the Great Basin bristlecone pine, a living monument that defies the boundaries of time itself. Methuselah takes its name from the biblical figure mentioned in the Hebrew Bible, who, according to Genesis, lived an astounding 969 years. This ancient tree has surpassed even the lifespan of its namesake.

For over an astounding 4,855 years, Methuselah has graced this Earth, dating back to when the ancient Egyptians meticulously crafted their timeless pyramids at Giza. Each passing year has etched a new chapter onto its majestic form, as if each ring on its weathered trunk is a page in a book, telling a story of survival, growth, and the wisdom that only millennia can bestow.

Imagine yourself standing before Methuselah, its branches stretching out like the arms of a celestial guardian. Its trunk, weathered by time, is a tapestry of intricate patterns, each one a testament to its endurance. The bark, a mosaic of deep browns and grays, bears the scars of countless storms and the sun's gentle caress. This living embodiment of strength and resilience is a testament to the enduring power of nature's creations.

Methuselah's longevity transcends the boundaries of our mortal existence. It invites us to contemplate the vastness of time and our interconnectedness with the Universe. Like Methuselah, we are intimately connected to the ebb and flow of the cosmic rhythm, drawing sustenance from the sacred embrace of the Earth. Just as Methuselah's roots delve deep into the soil, communing with the wisdom of ancient lands, our roots reach the depths of our consciousness, channeling the energy of countless experiences, thoughts, emotions, and beliefs. Like Methuselah's, these roots are our connection to the past, our source of strength and resilience.

In its presence, Methuselah invites us to pause, reflect upon the fleeting nature of our existence, and embrace the eternal essence that resides within. Just as Methuselah endures, grows, and leaves an indelible mark upon existence, our thoughts, emotions, and beliefs possess extraordinary power. As energetic vibrations, they radiate and intertwine within the expansive realm of the energetic field that envelops us.

Our interactions with this vast, energetic web, a network of interconnected energies, shape our experiences and journeys as we navigate life. Each thought carries its distinct frequency, each emotion ripples through the cosmic fabric, and each belief resonates throughout the Universe. We can harness this incredible power, attracting abundance and joy, fostering growth and connection, and leaving our unique mark upon the tapestry of existence. This web, like Methuselah, is a part of us, and we are a part of it, each thread contributing to the intricate design of our lives.

As we stand before Methuselah, the ancient tree that has witnessed the passage of time, we realize that our thoughts, emotions, and beliefs are akin to the essence of this enduring marvel. As its existence stretches across millennia, our inner world holds a vast reservoir of experiences, ideas, and perceptions that shape our reality.

THE RADIANT TRANSMITTERS: THOUGHTS AND THEIR FREQUENCIES SHAPING REALITY

The impact of thoughts on reality is a profound phenomenon. They shape our perceptions and interactions with the world and influence the experiences and outcomes we attract. Optimistic thoughts about our abilities empower us to approach challenges with confidence and resilience. This positive mindset opens doors to increased opportunities, better relationships, and success.

Conversely, self-limiting and negative thoughts impede progress and manifest undesirable outcomes. Dwelling on thoughts of failure, inadequacy, or fear unknowingly attracts situations that validate those beliefs, creating a vicious cycle. Our mindset can become a self-fulfilling prophecy, limiting our potential and preventing us from taking risks or seizing opportunities that could lead to growth and fulfillment.

It's crucial to recognize that thoughts are not fleeting or inconsequential. They generate energetic vibrations that interact with the Universe, influencing the circumstances and events in our lives. By cultivating a positive and empowering thought pattern, we align ourselves with frequencies that attract favorable outcomes and experiences.

To harness the influence of thoughts on reality, we must cultivate self-awareness and practice mindfulness. Observing our thoughts and consciously redirecting negative or unproductive thinking patterns can reshape our perception and actively shape our reality. Techniques such as affirmations, visualization, and gratitude practices are powerful tools for reprogramming and aligning our thoughts with the desired reality. We will explore these topics in more depth later in this book.

Understanding the impact of our thoughts on our reality grants us the ability to shape our experiences and create a life that aligns with our aspirations. Our thoughts act as seeds from which our reality grows, and by nurturing positive and empowering thoughts, we manifest a future filled with possibilities and fulfillment.

To better understand this concept, consider yourself a radio transmitter, sending signals into the expansive ether. Like that, our thoughts emit energetic frequencies that engage with the intricate fabric of vibrations that make up reality. Much like tuning in to a specific radio station, we can only experience the effects of a frequency if we attune to it.

Positive thoughts carry high-frequency vibrations of joy, inspiration, and love. When we align ourselves with such positive frequencies, we open ourselves to positive experiences and attract similar vibrations from the Universe. On the other hand, negative thoughts emit lower-frequency resonances characterized by fear, doubt, and negativity. These frequencies repel the experiences we desire, creating a discordant energetic field that hampers the manifestation of our goals.

> IN MANIFESTATION, WE ARE NOT PASSIVE
> OBSERVERS BUT ACTIVE PARTICIPANTS,
> WEAVING THE THREADS OF OUR CONSCIOUSNESS
> INTO THE FABRIC OF OUR REALITY

I want to share a personal experience that illustrates the power of thoughts and mindset. When I was nine, my school organized an orientation event in its grand auditorium. The room was excited as students and parents eagerly anticipated the start of the new school year. Parents engaged in animated conversations while children joyfully ran around, relishing the company of their friends. The atmosphere was electric, brimming with anticipation and energy.

While preparing for the orientation, the administrative assistant approached me, aware of my fluency in Khmer, and asked if I would deliver a special greeting on stage. I was assigned to say, "Hi, welcome to Euclid Elementary School! Thank you for being here, and we look forward to having you!" It was a beautiful concept that aimed to celebrate our diverse backgrounds by having students deliver greetings in their respective languages, fostering a sense of belonging and camaraderie before the official proceedings began.

Without a moment to collect my thoughts, my mother eagerly volunteered me for the opportunity. In that instant, a rush of overwhelming emotions swept over me, and fear tightened its grip on my heart. As a shy and introverted child, the mere thought of speaking in public would flood me with anxiety, causing waves of nervousness to course through my entire being. Adding to the pressure and nervousness was the knowledge that other students would also deliver greetings in their respective languages, intensifying my apprehension even further.

While fear and self-doubt threatened to consume me, a young Somali boy about my age exuded pure excitement and boundless energy. He confidently began rehearsing his lines, wholeheartedly embracing the attention.

"I got this, I got this!" he kept repeating, excitement in his voice.

With only thirty minutes to practice, my fear intensified with each passing second. The thought that I couldn't do it consumed my mind, urging me to give up. Despite practicing repeatedly, I struggled to articulate the words, rushing through them incoherently. The tension in my body grew as if anticipating an imminent threat.

I can't do this.
I can't do this.
I can't do this.

The mantra echoed relentlessly in my mind, fueling my unease. The weight of emotional strain and mounting pressure manifested physically, making me feel sick to my stomach. The desire to vomit welled up within me.

Fate designated me as the first child sacrifice, or so I felt. All eyes turned towards me, and my mind raced with self-doubt. A nervous smile stretched across my lips, but my mouth felt dry as I focused on a spot between my mother and another parent, unable to meet their expectant eyes. The room fell into an eerie silence. I could hear the pounding of my heartbeat.

My words spilled out in a rush, disjointed, and difficult to comprehend. It was over before I knew it, leaving me and everyone else in the room bewildered. The silence lingered for a moment, with people staring at me, waiting for more. But I had already stumbled through everything I had to say, lost in a jumble of gibberish.

Then, a woman's voice broke the silence with a sympathetic "Aww," followed by others. The realization of my blunder spread, and soon, pity-filled applause and laughter filled the room. I wanted nothing more than to disappear, to melt into the very stage beneath me.

Leaving the microphone behind, I made my way to the designated spot on stage, a wave of relief washing over me. The ordeal was finally over, but the embarrassment and humiliation remained etched in my memory.

Then came the Somali boy's turn. With a beaming smile, he approached the microphone, radiating confidence. He deliberately tried to establish eye contact with everyone he could. Holding his head high, he delivered his lines flawlessly, captivating the audience with his impeccable cadence. He paused as he concluded his performance, allowing the applause to wash over him. Rather than rushing back to his designated spot, he walked with an undeniable air of self-assurance, leaving a lasting impression on all who had witnessed his poised presence. He was splendid.

By allowing fear and self-doubt to dominate my thoughts, I unknowingly constructed barriers that prevented me from fully embracing the opportunity. The insecurities that consumed my mind created an atmosphere of self-doubt, suffocating my confidence and obscuring my true abilities. Consequently, my potential became stifled, and hindrances impeded my progress. The fear of making mistakes and becoming subject to ridicule kept me captive, preventing me from expressing myself genuinely and freely.

This experience served as a great lesson, revealing the immense power that our thoughts and mindsets hold in shaping our experiences and influencing the outcomes we achieve. It showcased the stark contrast between my classmate's positive thoughts and unwavering beliefs, which acted as a catalyst, propelling him forward with steadfast determination. Instead of viewing the challenge as an insurmountable obstacle, he embraced it as an opportunity for growth and personal triumph. Through cultivating positive thoughts and adopting a mindset of possibility, he harnessed his innate potential, unleashing it to its fullest extent.

Our thoughts transcend the realm of fleeting phenomena and hold immense power in shaping our reality. By cultivating self-awareness to gain a deeper understanding of our thought patterns, practicing mindfulness to remain present and focused, and consciously redirecting our thoughts toward positive and empowering perspectives, we can tap into our true potential and participate actively in co-creating our lives.

THE EMOTIONAL NAVIGATOR

Emotions are integral in shaping our reality, extending far beyond internal experiences. They act as our steadfast compass, influencing the intricate interplay of existence. Positive emotions like joy, gratitude, and love help harmonize our desires and intentions, paving the way for the manifestation of our sought-after experiences. On the other hand, negative emotions such as fear, doubt, and resentment introduce disharmony, hindering the realization of our desired outcomes.

To skillfully navigate the uncertainties of life, it is essential to embrace emotions as trustworthy guides wholeheartedly. By acknowledging and honoring our emotional landscape, we gain insight into the depths of our being. We can then recognize when fear may be holding us back, doubt clouding our judgment, or resentment poisoning our perspective. Through this awareness, we can consciously choose to transform negative emotions. Techniques such as mindfulness, cognitive reframing, or emotional freedom techniques can effectively align us with the positive energies that propel us forward.

The causes of emotional blockages are multifaceted. Traumatic experiences, such as abuse, neglect, accidents, or significant losses, can overwhelm our ability to process and express emotions, leading to the formation of emotional blockages. Additionally, childhood conditioning plays a crucial role. Messages received during our formative years about which emotions are acceptable or discouraged can shape our emotional responses. Cultural and societal influences, including gender norms and expectations, can further impact how we express and perceive emotions.

Inherited patterns also contribute to emotional blockages. Unresolved traumas and unhealed emotions from our ancestors can influence our emotional well-being, creating blockages that may persist across generations. Negative belief systems, such as feelings of unworthiness or undeservingness, can also contribute to developing emotional blockages. Lastly, fear and the need for self-protection can lead us to build walls around our emotions, inhibiting their natural flow.

Recognizing and addressing emotional blockages is crucial to healing and personal growth. We can identify and release these blockages through self-awareness, therapy, emotional healing techniques, and personal development practices. Doing so creates space for healthier emotional experiences, deeper connections with others, and a more fulfilling and authentic life journey.

> INHERITED PATTERNS AND SOCIETAL CONDITIONING SHAPE OUR EMOTIONAL LANDSCAPE—BUT WE HOLD THE POWER TO REWRITE OUR EMOTIONAL STORY.

As mentioned earlier, I was an introverted child. These aspects of my personality were influenced by various factors, such as childhood conditioning, inherited patterns, limiting beliefs, experiences of bullying, cultural and societal influences, and fear. Throughout my formative years, these influences operated subconsciously, casting a shadow over my daily life and creating a sense of disharmony that affected how I interacted with the world.

What I didn't realize then was that the emotions I carried within me emitted an energy that unconsciously pushed away potential opportunities and hindered my ability to form meaningful connections. This pattern unfolded automatically, without conscious thought or intention. These emotions impacted how I perceived and engaged with the world, ultimately limiting my experiences and impeding my personal growth well into adulthood.

An illustrative incident occurred at a gas station while I was in my twenties. That day, I found myself consumed by my negative emotional state, causing me to retreat inward. I deliberately avoided making eye contact with those around me, missing a valuable opportunity to strike up a conversation with someone who, unbeknownst to me then, would have played a pivotal role in my personal development. It was a missed connection that had significant consequences, and it took us five years to cross paths again, realizing the years of friendship we had lost. Reflecting on the situation, the person later revealed that my distant and hurried demeanor conveyed an impression of being unapproachable, further dissuading them from engaging with me.

In the workplace, my emotional blockages not only affected my performance but also hindered my ability to connect with others. These blockages manifested as a lack of confidence and engagement during meetings, which limited my capacity to make valuable contributions. Additionally, my reserved behavior prevented me from forming meaningful connections with my colleagues. As a result, the team needed more synergy to generate creative and innovative ideas, leading to stagnancy and setbacks in crucial projects.

Another instance where emotional blockages held sway over me occurred at the gym. During a workout, my eyes again remained averted because of fear of making eye contact, causing me to miss a golden opportunity. Unbeknownst to me, my favorite comedian, Dave Chappelle, was working out in the same area. In a strange twist of fate, we were the only two people present for nearly a half hour, yet I remained oblivious to his presence until someone pointed it out after he had departed. It was a missed opportunity to start a conversation and form a positive memory.

Looking back, I can't help but feel that my memories of the past were dull and lifeless as if I were stuck in a monochromatic world. In contrast, I have undergone a remarkable transformation, shifting my emotional perspective and cultivating a positive mindset. This change is an ongoing and intentional process that begins before I step out of bed each morning.

I greet each new day with enthusiasm and gratitude, recognizing it as a precious gift. This proactive approach primes my emotional state, infusing it with harmony and positivity. As I venture into the world, my energized and optimistic mindset becomes like a magnet, radiating vibrant energy that attracts opportunities and encounters perfectly aligned with my optimistic outlook.

One day, while shopping at a home store, I had a chance encounter with the store owner. Now unafraid to make eye contact, I said hello and stuck up a conversation with him. It turned out that he needed someone with expertise in my field. This unexpected meeting led to a new client relationship, demonstrating how a simple interaction can lead to exciting professional opportunities.

This transformation in my emotional state also had a tremendous impact on my professional endeavors. The radiance of my positive energy permeated my work environment, changing the dynamics of my interactions. My colleagues were naturally drawn to my contagious enthusiasm, fostering a sense of unity and collaboration within our team. This harmonious synergy nurtured an environment where creative ideas flourished and innovation thrived. Together, we created a culture of openness and shared vision, paving the way for successful outcomes across various projects. As a result, I formed strong professional relationships and developed close friendships with my colleagues, as our shared passion and drive brought us closer together.

One evening, fueled by a burning desire to reshape the past, I poured my emotions and intentions onto the pages of my journal. With unwavering determination, I expressed my deep desire to cross paths with Dave Chappelle again, fully aware that the version of myself at that moment was primed for such an extraordinary encounter. Treating this aspiration as a shopping list or a task to be accomplished, I set the wheels of manifestation in motion.

While enjoying brunch with a dear friend the next day, our conversation naturally gravitated toward manifestation. Seizing the opportune moment, I casually shared my remarkable intention to manifest a meeting with Dave Chappelle that day. To our astonishment, as if orchestrated by some unseen cosmic conductor, the comedian immediately appeared just a few feet away from us. The unexpected presence left us in awe, marveling at the synchronicity of my manifestation.

These examples vividly illustrate the immense power of our

emotions in shaping our daily experiences. By consciously cultivating a positive emotional state and maintaining an optimistic outlook, we can rewrite our programming and create lives filled with meaningful connections, exciting opportunities, and personal fulfillment.

BELIEFS:
BLUEPRINTS THAT BUILD OUR REALITY

Beliefs serve as the blueprints that shape our reality, influencing how we perceive the world and guiding our actions. They possess significant power, as they can unlock our highest potential or create barriers that hinder our fulfillment and aspirations.

During my upbringing, I found myself entangled in a web of restrictive beliefs that held me back. As a first-generation American, my immigrant parents escaped the horrors of the Khmer Rouge, which left them with post-traumatic stress disorder and limiting beliefs. Their struggles and high expectations burdened me with an overwhelming sense of responsibility. The pressure to excel academically and in extracurricular activities took a toll on my well-being and mental health.

Positive feedback was scarce, while critiques were predominantly negative. Phrases like "You always make mistakes. Can't you do anything right?" or "Is that all you can do? You need to try harder" became all too familiar. These words became deeply ingrained beliefs that shaped how I saw myself. The message was clear: *You are not good enough.*

Encounters with bullies at school intensified these beliefs, fostering a subconscious belief of inadequacy. This belief system constrained my actions, leading to self-sabotage and missed opportunities. I settled for mediocrity, convinced I didn't deserve more significant achievements. This cycle of stagnation and unfulfilled potential persisted into my early adulthood, affecting all areas of my life.

> RECOGNIZING THE ORIGINS OF OUR LIMITING BELIEFS IS THE FIRST STEP TOWARDS REWRITING THE NARRATIVE AND RECLAIMING OUR POWER.

These limiting beliefs heavily influenced my career choices, causing me to accept positions that undervalued my skills and failed to recognize my true worth. Doubting my abilities, I settled for roles that offered limited opportunities for growth or personal satisfaction. These beliefs prevented me from pursuing more challenging and fulfilling paths that could have propelled me toward success.

My beliefs about love also significantly shaped my experiences. I settled for relationships and circumstances that didn't bring me genuine fulfillment, convinced that I didn't deserve better or that superior options were unavailable. Consequently, I remained in unhealthy or unsupportive relationships, depriving myself of the chance to seek and nurture connections that could have brought genuine happiness and emotional well-being.

These limiting beliefs extended into other areas of my life, including health and fitness, intelligence, learning, hobbies, and finance. They created barriers to success, impeding my progress and personal growth.

On the other hand, I had a close friend from middle school who strongly believed in himself and his abilities. Free from the hardships I experienced, he exuded confidence and determination. His empowering beliefs fueled his pursuit of a medical career, aligning with his self-worth and recognition of his talents. This unshakeable belief in himself propelled his academic excellence, enabling him to persevere through the challenges of medical school and emerge triumphant.

In matters of love, he actively sought and nurtured connections that brought him genuine fulfillment. Refusing to settle for anything less, he believed in his worthiness and was unafraid to walk away from situations that didn't align with his needs.

This empowering belief system had a ripple effect in all areas of his life. He wholeheartedly embraced personal growth, recognizing its importance in his journey. With an unwavering belief in himself and his abilities, he pursued his passions wholeheartedly, refusing to settle for mediocrity. He prioritized his well-being, understanding that his happiness and fulfillment were essential. This mindset propelled him to make incredible strides in all areas of life, achieving success, joy, and personal satisfaction.

Recognizing the immense influence of beliefs empowers us to redesign our lives. It is a transformative journey that requires determination, self-reflection, and intentional reprogramming of our thought patterns. By dismantling limiting beliefs and cultivating empowering ones, we expand the boundaries of what we believe is possible.

The journey of belief transformation is ongoing. It is not a destination but a continuous process of self-discovery and learning. As we challenge and redefine our beliefs, we open ourselves to new possibilities and opportunities. We gain a deeper understanding of our capabilities, strengths, and worthiness.

The impact of our belief transformation extends beyond our individual lives. As we reshape our beliefs and choose to live in alignment with our true potential, we inspire and influence others around us. Our positive energy, actions, and achievements can radiate into our communities and society, creating a collective reality that embraces growth, empowerment, and positive change.

PART II
the steps

"You are not a drop in the ocean.
You are the entire ocean in a drop."

RUMI

Step 1:

SELF-LOVE AND SELF-WORTH

DEVELOPING A SOLID sense of self-love and self-worth is the fundamental key to manifestation, as it shapes an authentic and fulfilling life beyond surface-level personal growth. In today's society, there is often an excessive focus on seeking external validation through achievements, appearances, and societal standards. This emphasis can cause us to overlook the importance of tending to our inner selves.

True self-love and self-worth originate from within and are independent of external circumstances or others' opinions. They arise from recognizing and accepting our inherent value as human beings. By acknowledging that we deserve love, respect, and happiness simply by existing, we align ourselves with the energy of abundance and unconditional love.

When we lack a sense of wholeness within ourselves, we emit an energy of lack that hinders manifestation. However, by cultivating self-love and self-worth and working on our internal dialogue, we bridge this gap and dissolve the energy of lack, creating fertile ground for manifestation to flourish. This process of self-acceptance and positive inner work is essential for aligning our vibration with our desired outcomes.

Harnessing the transformative power of self-love and self-worth makes manifesting our dreams possible. Believing in our worthiness magnetizes opportunities, relationships, and circumstances that align with our wishes. Self-love and self-worth catalyze positive change and growth, empowering us to create a fulfilling life.

J.K. Rowling, the acclaimed author of the beloved *Harry Potter* series, provides an inspiring example of embracing this concept through her remarkable journey. At the time of writing, Rowling has sold over 600 million copies of her books worldwide. Her extraordinary success is a testament to the profound impact of recognizing and nurturing one's value.

In the early stages of her writing career, Rowling faced numerous rejections from publishers who failed to recognize the value and potential of her work. Despite these setbacks, Rowling maintained a strong belief in her story and nurtured herself with self-love and self-worth. She refused to let the opinions of others diminish her passion and conviction.

Throughout her challenging journey, Rowling embraced her self-worth and remained steadfast in her belief that her writing held immense value. She recognized that her worth as a writer extended beyond the judgments and rejections she encountered.

Eventually, Bloomsbury, a publishing house in the United Kingdom, saw the potential in Rowling's work and took a chance on her. In 1997, J.K. Rowling published the first *Harry Potter* book, quickly captivating readers worldwide. Rowling's unwavering self-love and belief in her worth as an author had paid off.

As the *Harry Potter* series gained unprecedented success, Rowling's self-love and self-worth flourished. She used her platform to advocate for important causes, such as literacy and children's rights, demonstrating her deep understanding of her value and the impact she could make on the world.

Rowling's journey from rejection to worldwide acclaim showcases the power of perseverance and emphasizes the significance of nurturing oneself with love. Rowling defied the critics by valuing herself and her talents and proved that true worth comes from within.

Her story serves as an inspiring reminder that embracing our self-worth and nurturing ourselves with self-love can empower us to overcome obstacles, achieve outstanding success, and make a positive impact on the lives of others.

SELF-LOVE AND SELF-WORTH REQUIRE CHALLENGING SOCIETAL NARRATIVES THAT UNDERMINE OUR SENSE OF VALUE AND SHIFTING OUR FOCUS FROM EXTERNAL VALIDATION TO CULTIVATING DEEP SELF-ACCEPTANCE.

The journey toward self-love and self-worth involves challenging societal narratives and cultural conditioning that might undermine our sense of value. It requires shifting our focus from seeking external validation to cultivating deep self-acceptance and self-appreciation. This process involves recognizing and embracing our strengths, vulnerabilities, imperfections, and unique qualities that make us who we are.

When we develop self-love and self-worth, we free ourselves from needing constant validation and approval from others. We learn to define our worth based on our internal compass and values. This newfound sense of self allows us to make choices that align with our authentic selves and bring us joy and fulfillment.

Self-love and self-worth are essential for successful manifestation in various areas of our lives. When we genuinely believe in our worthiness, we attract positive experiences and opportunities. By embodying self-love and self-worth, we radiate a positive energy that draws abundance and happiness into our lives.

The path of self-love and self-worth is a complex and transformative journey. It demands an unwavering commitment to self-reflection, introspection, and self-care. It compels us to confront and reshape the damaging narratives of negative self-talk and limiting beliefs that have become deeply ingrained. It calls for the practice of self-compassion and forgiveness as we navigate the intricate terrain of our imperfections and the shadows of past mistakes.

NURTURING SELF-LOVE AND SELF-WORTH THROUGH SELF-CARE PRACTICES

Practicing self-love and cultivating self-worth are transformative journeys that require intentional actions and care. They involve promoting physical, mental, and emotional well-being beyond mere indulgence. By committing to regular self-care practices, we affirm our deservingness of love, attention, and care, establishing a foundation for cultivating self-love and self-worth.

- **PHYSICAL SELF-CARE**

   Regular exercise, physical activities, and balanced nutrition can improve our physical health, mood, and stress levels. Simple practices like walking, hiking, swimming, dancing, or participating in sports can boost our cardiovascular fitness, muscle strength, and flexibility. Fueling our bodies with wholesome, nutrient-dense foods, staying hydrated, and regularly checking in with healthcare providers are also crucial for maintaining physical well-being.

- **REST**

   Prioritizing quality sleep and rest is crucial for rejuvenating our minds and bodies. Establishing a consistent sleep routine, creating a peaceful sleep environment free from blue light and distractions, and practicing relaxation techniques like deep breathing, meditation, or gentle stretching can facilitate better sleep. Taking breaks throughout the day to step away from work or daily demands, scheduling regular downtime, and engaging in unwinding activities such as reading, listening to soothing music, or spending time in nature are also crucial for managing stress and maintaining life balance.

- **EMOTIONAL WELL-BEING**

  Acknowledging and healthily processing our emotions is vital for our overall well-being. Practices like journaling, therapy or counseling, and creative outlets such as art, music, or writing can provide avenues for emotional expression and support. Setting healthy boundaries, learning to say no when necessary, and surrounding ourselves with positive, supportive relationships are vital for prioritizing our emotional health.

- **SELF-COMPASSION AND SELF-KINDNESS**

  Treating ourselves with kindness, understanding, and patience, especially during challenges, is essential to self-love. Embracing self-forgiveness, celebrating our strengths and accomplishments, and using positive self-talk and affirmations can cultivate self-compassion. Practicing self-care rituals, like taking a relaxing bath or engaging in activities that bring us joy, can also nurture self-compassion.

- **JOYFUL ACTIVITIES**

  Engaging in hobbies, creative pursuits, and activities that bring us fulfillment and relaxation can profoundly impact our overall well-being. Exploring new interests, such as learning a new skill, language, or hobby, can reignite our sense of curiosity and wonder. Spending time in nature, whether on a stroll, a hike, or simply observing the surrounding beauty, can have a calming and restorative effect on our minds and bodies. Connecting with loved ones through shared experiences, such as game nights, movie marathons, or shared meals, can also contribute to our joy and connection.

Engaging in self-care establishes a strong foundation for fostering self-love and self-worth. Taking intentional steps to nurture ourselves creates a solid base for personal growth, happiness, and overall well-being. The above practices allow us to cultivate self-love and self-worth, navigate challenges, and gracefully develop resilience.

> OUR CAPACITY TO LOVE AND BELIEVE IN OURSELVES IS THE MASTER KEY TO UNLOCKING OUR GREATEST POSSIBILITIES.

THE POWER OF SELF-COMPASSION

Self-compassion is a vital aspect of nurturing self-love and self-worth. It teaches us to shift our perspective from self-criticism to kindness, understanding, and forgiveness. Instead of berating ourselves for perceived failures, self-compassion invites us to embrace our imperfections and recognize our shared humanity. It encourages us to offer ourselves the same support and understanding we would extend to a dear friend facing challenges.

When we practice self-compassion, we develop a nurturing inner dialogue. We become more aware of our thoughts and emotions, responding with gentle encouragement and self-care. This practice allows us to validate our feelings without judgment, creating space for healing, growth, and learning from our experiences.

Cultivating self-compassion also involves building a loving relationship with ourselves. It means treating ourselves with care, respect, and empathy. It includes prioritizing our needs, setting healthy boundaries, and engaging in self-care rituals that nourish our physical, mental, and emotional well-being. It entails acknowledging our strengths, celebrating our achievements, and embracing self-acceptance in our triumphs and vulnerabilities.

By practicing self-compassion, we create a safe and nurturing environment within ourselves. We develop resilience and the ability to bounce back from setbacks with kindness and understanding. This practice fosters deep self-love and self-worth, laying a solid foundation for personal growth, happiness, and well-being.

EMBRACE WHO YOU ARE

Self-acceptance forms a fundamental pillar in nurturing self-love and self-worth. It transcends mere acknowledgment of our positive qualities, inviting us to embrace every facet of our being wholeheartedly. By embracing self-acceptance, we are encouraged to welcome our strengths, weaknesses, quirks, and past mistakes with compassion and understanding, liberating ourselves from judgment or resistance.

Embracing self-acceptance should not be misconstrued as settling for mediocrity or complacency. Instead, it involves a profound recognition of our authentic selves in the present moment, accompanied by acts of self-kindness and understanding. It necessitates an acknowledgment of our imperfections and inherent humanity, liberating us from the notion that achievements or failures solely determine our worth.

An example of self-acceptance lies in embracing our strengths and talents while refusing to downplay or compare them. It involves acknowledging and celebrating our unique abilities and cherishing the qualities that define us. I nurtured ideas for years about writing this book. However, I initially harbored fears of not being good enough (from childhood, which I discussed in Chapter 2) and concerns that the world would not accept my work. Through self-acceptance, I embraced my true self, letting go of apprehension regarding others' perceptions. It enabled me to value and express my creative gift, free from external standards. I found the courage to embrace my authentic voice and fearlessly share my story, unencumbered by the world's judgments.

Self-acceptance also encompasses a profound awareness of our weaknesses and areas of growth. It requires us to embrace our imperfections and acknowledge that perfection is unattainable. Instead of criticizing ourselves for perceived shortcomings, self-acceptance encourages us to approach these areas with curiosity, compassion, and a growth mindset. Consider the example of my nine-year-old self, who grappled with a fear of public speaking. Self-acceptance eventually allowed me to recognize this challenge without self-judgment, paving the way for seeking opportunities to develop and grow in that domain.

Self-acceptance beckons us to embrace our quirks and idiosyncrasies, acknowledging and celebrating the aspects of ourselves that may not conform to societal expectations or pressures to fit in. It is an invitation to honor our individuality and find solace in the authenticity of our being.

> LOVING YOURSELF, FLAWS AND ALL,
> IS THE TRUEST PATH TO WHOLENESS.

Moreover, self-acceptance entails embracing and extracting valuable lessons from our past mistakes. It necessitates acknowledging that errors are inherent in our human experience, and forgiveness for our choices is essential. I once struggled to forgive myself for stumbling in that auditorium during my younger years, resulting in heightened self-criticism. However, through self-acceptance, I have come to terms with my past, recognizing it as a valuable learning experience. This process allows us to let go of shame and self-judgment, replacing them with self-compassion and a growth mindset.

Self-acceptance encompasses embracing all facets of our being—strengths, weaknesses, quirks, and past mistakes. It involves recognizing and embracing the truth of our identity without judgment or resistance. Through self-acceptance, we can celebrate our unique qualities, grow from life's challenges, and cultivate a profound sense of self-love and self-worth.

PRACTICAL EXERCISES AND TECHNIQUES FOR SELF-LOVE AND SELF-WORTH

Engaging in practical exercises and techniques is essential for nurturing self-love and self-worth. Implementing this empowers us to develop acceptance, appreciation, and confidence while providing valuable tools to shift our mindset, challenge negative self-perceptions, and embrace our inherent worthiness. With dedicated effort and commitment, we can transform ourselves and foster a loving and positive relationship with ourselves.

- **AFFIRMATIONS**

  Affirmations possess the transformative power to shape our inner dialogue. Through the conscious selection and repetition of positive affirmations, we can reframe our mindset, challenge self-doubt, and construct a solid foundation of acceptance and appreciation within ourselves.

  – I deserve love and respect, just as I am.
  – I embrace my unique qualities and celebrate what makes me

special."

- I am enough and worthy of all the good things life offers.
- I love and accept myself unconditionally.
- I am worthy of happiness, success, and fulfillment.
- I am worthy of love and healthy, supportive relationships.
- I radiate confidence and believe in my abilities.
- I trust myself to make the best decisions for my well-being.
- I forgive myself for past mistakes and embrace growth.

It is essential to choose affirmations that deeply resonate with you and make them a regular part of your life. Let these affirmations guide you toward cultivating self-compassion and a fulfilling relationship with yourself. With dedication and practice, affirmations can transform your journey of self-love and self-worth.

VISUALIZATION

Visualization is a powerful practice that can support self-love and self-worth. By creating vivid mental images of ourselves as confident, empowered, and deserving individuals, we access the creative power of our minds and send a clear message to the Universe about the reality we wish to manifest. Through visualization, we can embody the feelings of self-love and self-worth, making them more tangible and present in our daily lives.

MIRROR VISUALIZATION AFFIRMATIONS

Stand in front of a mirror and visualize yourself radiating self-love and self-worth. Look into your own eyes and repeat positive affirmations about yourself, such as "I am worthy of love and respect," "I embrace my uniqueness," or "I am deserving of happiness." Visualize these affirmations sinking into your subconscious mind, reinforcing your sense of self-worth.

— FUTURE-SELF VISUALIZATION

Close your eyes and imagine your ideal future self, the person you aspire to be. Visualize yourself embodying self-love and self-worth in every aspect of your life. See yourself engaging in activities that bring you joy and fulfillment, surrounded by loving relationships, and thriving in your chosen endeavors. By visualizing this upbeat future version of yourself, you can strengthen your belief in your worthiness.

— INNER CHILD VISUALIZATION

Imagine yourself as a child, with all your vulnerabilities, innocence, and potential. Visualize yourself extending love, compassion, and acceptance to your inner child. Picture yourself embracing that child version of yourself, offering reassurance and unconditional love. This visualization can help heal past wounds and cultivate deep self-love and self-worth.

— SELF-APPRECIATION VISUALIZATION

Take a few moments to reflect on your positive qualities, achievements, and strengths. Close your eyes and visualize a montage of these qualities, accomplishments, and moments of personal growth. Feel the sense of pride and self-appreciation wash over you as you immerse yourself in this visualization. Focusing on your strengths and acknowledging your accomplishments can strengthen your self-worth.

Visualization is a powerful tool for reinforcing positive self-perceptions and manifesting a reality rooted in self-love and self-worth. By integrating visualization practices into our daily routines, we can transform our inner dialogue, nurture our sense of worthiness, and embrace a more loving and positive relationship with ourselves. Through the creative power of visualization, we open ourselves up to a world of possibilities where self-love and self-worth are at the core of our being.

- **JOURNALING**

  Journaling is a powerful practice. Putting our thoughts, feelings, and experiences into writing gives us invaluable clarity and insight into our inner world. It provides a safe and nurturing space for self-expression and self-reflection, allowing us to identify and challenge self-limiting beliefs, reflect on our achievements and strengths, and cultivate gratitude for our journey. Regular journaling deepens our understanding of ourselves, challenges negative self-perceptions, and fosters a greater sense of self-love and self-worth.

  - **SELF-REFLECTION**

    Take time to write about your thoughts, emotions, and experiences. Explore your fears, doubts, and insecurities, as well as your dreams, aspirations, and accomplishments. Reflect on the challenges you've overcome and the lessons you've learned. Use your journal as a tool for self-discovery and self-acceptance. By delving into your inner world, you can uncover hidden strengths and develop a more compassionate understanding of yourself.

— GRATITUDE JOURNALING

Dedicate a section of your journal to gratitude. Write things you appreciate about yourself, your strengths, and the positive aspects of your life. Express gratitude for the qualities that make you unique and your progress on your journey towards self-love. Cultivating gratitude can shift your focus towards self-appreciation and foster a more positive outlook. Making gratitude journaling a habit can help rewire your brain to focus on the good, even during challenging times.

— AFFIRMATION JOURNALING

Write affirmations that resonate with you and reinforce self-love and self-worth. Repeat these affirmations daily and write about the emotions and sensations they evoke within you. Reflect on how these positive statements impact your self-perception and mindset. Affirmation journaling can be a powerful tool for reprogramming negative thought patterns and building a stronger self-belief.

— LETTER TO SELF

Write a heartfelt letter to yourself, expressing love, compassion, and encouragement. Offer words of kindness and support, acknowledging your worthiness and potential. This exercise allows you to cultivate self-compassion and remind yourself of your value. Reading back on these letters can be a profound source of comfort and motivation during self-doubt or struggle.

— CELEBRATING ACHIEVEMENTS

Use your journal to celebrate your accomplishments, both big and small. Write about challenges you have overcome, goals you have achieved, and personal growth you have experienced. Reflect on the strengths and qualities that contributed to your success, reinforcing a sense of self-worth. Celebrating your wins, no matter how seemingly insignificant, can boost your confidence and inspire you to keep progressing on your self-love journey.

By engaging in regular journaling practices, you can deepen your understanding of yourself, challenge negative self-perceptions, and foster a greater sense of self-love and self-worth. Journaling provides a powerful outlet for self-expression and self-reflection, supporting your journey toward embracing your authentic self and cultivating a positive relationship with yourself.

▪ REAL-LIFE INSPIRATIONS

Seeking inspiration from real-life examples of individuals who have nurtured self-love and self-worth can be powerful. If you struggle with feelings of unworthiness, find someone you admire who exudes confidence and emulate their behavior, mindset, and actions. Observe their posture, body language, and communication style, incorporating those qualities into your behavior. Study their empowering beliefs and positive self-talk, adapting them for yourself. Remember to stay true to your values and engage in self-reflection and inner work to cultivate your unique self-love and self-worth.

Additionally, consider seeking supportive communities, either in person or online, where you can connect with others who prioritize self-love. Sharing your experiences and learning from each other can deepen your understanding of this transformative process.

Nurturing self-love and self-worth is an ongoing process that requires consistent effort, patience, and self-compassion as we navigate life's challenges. While we may experience regression into old patterns of self-doubt or self-criticism, it's essential to approach ourselves with kindness and understanding. Self-love and self-worth are lifelong journeys that evolve and deepen.

Cultivating self-love and self-worth is vital for manifesting success and fulfilling life. As we develop these essential qualities, we align ourselves with abundance and attract positive experiences and opportunities. This empowering mindset shapes our reality, enabling us to live authentically and achieve our deepest desires. Cultivating self-acceptance and self-belief becomes a potent catalyst, empowering us to show up courageously and create the rewarding existence we are meant to live.

OVERCOME SUBCONSCIOUS LIMITING BELIEFS AND RESISTANCE

"Your subconscious mind is like a garden and your thoughts are the seeds. You can choose to plant flowers or weeds."

UNKNOWN

Step 2:

OVERCOME SUBCONSCIOUS LIMITING BELIEFS AND RESISTANCE

"I think I can, I can," echoes in my mind whenever I think of subconscious limiting beliefs and resistance. The quote originates from the beloved children's story *The Little Engine That Could*, written by Watty Piper.

In this heartwarming tale, a small and determined train engine takes on the formidable challenge of pulling a heavy load of toys and goods over a steep mountain. Along its journey, the little engine faces doubts and resistance from larger, more powerful engines refusing assistance.

Undeterred by skepticism and whispers of doubt, the little engine gathers its courage and resolves to face the challenge head-on. With every chug, its mantra echoes through the hills, "I think I can, I think I can." These simple words become a powerful affirmation, challenging the limiting beliefs that threaten to hold it back.

With unwavering determination and a shift in mindset, the little engine embarks on its ascent. It pushes through the weight of the cargo and down the steep incline, defying the odds. Slowly but steadily, it conquers the mountain, achieving what others had deemed impossible. Its triumph becomes a testament to the incredible power of overcoming subconscious limiting beliefs and resistance.

This story stands as a timeless metaphor for the strength of optimism, perseverance, and the courage to challenge the limitations we impose upon ourselves. It imparts a valuable lesson about cultivating a positive mindset, nurturing self-belief, and forging ahead despite the resistance we may encounter. This delightful story inspires us to embrace our journeys, arming us with the conviction that wholeheartedly believing in ourselves enables us to surmount any obstacle and bring our dreams to fruition.

Subconscious limiting beliefs take shape through myriad factors, experiences, and influences that leave an indelible mark on our psyche. During our formative years, childhood experiences wield tremendous power, as negative events, criticism, and the repetitive messages we receive from authority figures mold our self-perception and worldview. Additionally, cultural and societal norms, saturated with stereotypes and expectations, can contribute to beliefs that confine us within predetermined gender roles, narrow career choices, or restrictive social statuses.

The process of conditioning and reinforcement further cements these limiting beliefs within our subconscious. Our minds absorb and internalize experiences that align with our existing beliefs, effectively solidifying their hold over us. As we stumble through personal setbacks and failures, especially when they become recurrent, a sense of incapability or unworthiness can take root, impairing our ability to embrace our full potential. External influences, such as the media's portrayal of beauty and success, can insidiously shape our beliefs, distorting our sense of what is genuinely possible for ourselves.

Yet, amidst this labyrinth of limiting beliefs lies hope. By undertaking self-discovery and awareness, we can challenge the validity of these beliefs. We can confront the subjective nature of our interpretations, realizing that they are not grounded in objective truth. Through this realization, we can reshape our beliefs, liberating ourselves from their confining grasp.

It is crucial to recognize that reshaping our beliefs requires conscious effort. By shining a light on our subconscious, we can identify the beliefs that no longer serve us and replace them with empowering alternatives. With each step forward, we align our beliefs with our goals and aspirations, embracing a newfound sense of empowerment and possibility.

In this transformative space, we unveil that our limiting beliefs are not insurmountable barriers. They are malleable constructs that can be dismantled and replaced with empowering beliefs. By challenging the validity of our limiting beliefs and replacing them with truths that resonate with our authentic selves, we pave the way for personal growth, resilience, and fulfilling our deepest aspirations.

SELF-REFLECTION AND CULTIVATE AWARENESS

Engaging in self-reflection and cultivating awareness is crucial for overcoming subconscious limiting beliefs. By dedicating time to journaling and self-reflection, we can identify and examine negative thought patterns that hinder our progress. This process gives us insights into our beliefs, thoughts, and self-talk.

For instance, I once struggled with self-doubt and fear of failure in my career. By journaling, I discovered recurring negative self-talk, such as "I'm not talented enough" or "I'll never achieve my goals." This self-reflection made me aware of the limiting beliefs rooted in experiences and comparisons to others.

Once we become aware of these limiting beliefs, we can challenge and reframe them. It's essential to question their validity and seek evidence that contradicts them. By dismantling the foundation of our limiting beliefs, we can replace them with empowering and supportive thoughts.

Cultivating awareness throughout our daily lives is vital. By paying attention to our thoughts, emotions, and reactions, we can catch ourselves engaging in negative self-talk or falling into the trap of limiting beliefs. Mindfulness practices, such as meditation or breathing exercises, can help develop this awareness.

Practicing self-compassion and non-judgment is crucial in this process. Instead of criticizing ourselves, we should approach our limiting beliefs with kindness and curiosity. Embracing the journey of self-discovery and growth, we recognize that every step toward awareness brings us closer to liberation from our self-imposed limitations.

> ENGAGING IN SELF-REFLECTION AND CULTIVATING
> AWARENESS ALLOWS US TO CHALLENGE
> AND REFRAME OUR LIMITING BELIEFS,
> REPLACING THEM WITH EMPOWERING THOUGHTS.

Remember to approach this process with self-compassion and curiosity. Acknowledging awareness fosters personal growth and transformation, leading us toward realizing our true potential.

1. DEDICATE SPECIFIC TIME TO JOURNALING AND SELF-REFLECTION

Take the time to journal and engage in self-reflection regularly. This dedicated practice deepens your self-awareness and understanding. Set aside specific moments in your day or week to express your thoughts, feelings, and experiences in writing. Use this opportunity to delve into your inner world, gaining insights and clarity about yourself.

2. **EXPLORE YOUR BELIEFS, THOUGHTS, AND SELF-TALK**

Take a closer look at the beliefs, thoughts, and self-talk limiting you. Identify areas in which you feel restricted or held back. By exploring these aspects, you open yourself to a more profound self-understanding. Recognize the patterns and narratives that shape your perception of yourself and your abilities.

3. **CHALLENGE LIMITING BELIEFS AND FOSTER EMPOWERING MINDSETS**

Actively challenge the validity of your limiting beliefs. Seek evidence that contradicts these beliefs and supports a more empowering mindset. Look for examples of your achievements, strengths, and positive experiences that go against the limitations you've imposed on yourself. This process helps you cultivate a mindset that empowers and uplifts you.

4. **CULTIVATE AWARENESS IN YOUR DAILY LIFE**

Cultivate awareness by consciously paying attention to your thoughts, emotions, and reactions throughout the day. Notice how certain situations or interactions trigger specific responses within you. This heightened awareness enhances your self-understanding and promotes personal growth. Take moments to reflect on your experiences and learn from them.

5. **EMBRACE SELF-COMPASSION AND NON-JUDGMENT**

Embrace self-compassion as you traverse this transformative journey. Practice non-judgment and accept yourself with kindness and understanding. Be gentle with yourself when faced with challenges or areas of improvement. Treat yourself with the same compassion as a friend or family member. This self-compassion creates a nurturing environment for growth.

6. **REMEMBER THE GRADUAL PROCESS OF CHANGE**

Change is a gradual process. Patience and persistence are key. Each step you take forward, no matter how small, contributes to your personal growth and transformation. Trust in the journey and believe in your ability to evolve and become the person you aspire to be. Embrace the learning and growth that comes with each experience along the way.

By following these steps and embracing the journey, we can cultivate our capabilities and unlock new possibilities. Patience, persistence, and belief in ourselves are essential as we learn, grow, and expand the boundaries of what we believe to be achievable. With this mindset, we can move beyond limiting perceptions and step into an empowered state of being.

CHALLENGE AND REFRAME LIMITING BELIEFS

By cultivating awareness of your limiting beliefs, you open the door to questioning their validity and understanding how they affect your advancement. Once you bring these beliefs to the forefront of your consciousness, you can actively challenge them. You begin to scrutinize the evidence supporting them and seek instances where you have experienced success or received positive feedback. This inquiry and exploration process provides valuable insights into the origins and impact of these limiting beliefs. As a result, you gain the power to consciously select more empowering thoughts and perspectives that support your growth and success.

Continuing with my previous story, I became aware of and identified my limiting beliefs that I wasn't talented enough and would never accomplish my goals. Now, it was time for me to question and challenge these beliefs. I started by asking myself why I believed I wasn't good enough or couldn't achieve my goals. Was there concrete evidence supporting these beliefs, or were they merely based on self-criticism or comparison to others? It became clear that the belief lacked substantial evidence.

To counteract this belief, I actively sought contrary evidence. I reflected on instances where I had succeeded or received positive feedback from others. I recalled past accomplishments, personal growth, and positive experiences related to my goals. I reminded myself of times when I overcame challenges or achieved things I initially thought were impossible. This contrary evidence played a significant role in dismantling the limiting beliefs that had held me back. Revisiting these positive experiences was genuinely empowering.

With heightened awareness of my internal dialogue, I finally became prepared to actively replace negative self-talk with positive and empowering affirmations and statements. Whenever I thought, "I'm not talented enough," I consciously challenged that thought by affirming my capabilities and strengths. I reminded myself of my unique qualities and past achievements, reinforcing the belief that I could achieve great things. By actively embracing positive self-talk and nurturing empowering thoughts, I created a mental landscape supporting my growth and success.

> CONFRONTING YOUR DEEPEST INSECURITIES HEAD-ON IS THE ONLY WAY TO TRANSCEND THE BARRIERS THEY CREATE.

AFFIRMATIONS

Affirmations are powerful statements or mantras that reinforce positive beliefs, thoughts, and self-perceptions, countering negative self-talk and fostering a positive mindset. Regular repetition enables us to reprogram our subconscious mind by replacing self-limiting beliefs with empowering thoughts. Positive affirmations have numerous benefits, including boosting self-confidence, enhancing self-esteem, and cultivating an optimistic outlook.

As I challenged and reframed my limiting beliefs, I armed myself with affirmations to combat them head-on. Instead of succumbing to thoughts like "I'm not talented enough," I embraced affirmations such as "I am more than enough and fully capable of achieving great things." Gradually, these affirmations replaced my negative self-talk and empowered me to embrace my true potential.

- **LIMITING BELIEF:** I am not smart enough to succeed.

  AFFIRMATION: I am intelligent and capable of learning and achieving anything I set my mind to.

- **LIMITING BELIEF:** I am unworthy of love.

  AFFIRMATION: I deserve love, respect, and nurturing relationships. I attract positive and loving people into my life.

- **LIMITING BELIEF:** Money is hard to come by, and I will never be financially secure.

  AFFIRMATION: I am open to receiving abundance and wealth. Money flows freely and easily into my life, and I am financially secure.

- **LIMITING BELIEF:** I am not talented enough to pursue my passions and succeed.

  AFFIRMATION: I possess unique talents and abilities. I confidently pursue my passions, and success follows me everywhere.

- **LIMITING BELIEF:** I am undeserving of happiness and joy.

  AFFIRMATION: I am worthy of happiness and joy. I embrace positivity and allow myself to experience deep fulfillment and contentment.

- **LIMITING BELIEF:** I am unlucky, and things never work out.

  AFFIRMATION: I am a magnet for good fortune and opportunities. Life aligns with my desires, and I attract positive outcomes.

- **LIMITING BELIEF:** I am too old/young to pursue my dreams.

  AFFIRMATION: My age is irrelevant to my dreams and aspirations. I am capable and empowered to pursue my passions at any stage of life.

- **LIMITING BELIEF:** Failure is inevitable, and I will never succeed.

  AFFIRMATION: I embrace failure as an opportunity for growth and learning. With each setback, I become stronger and closer to achieving my goals.

- **LIMITING BELIEF:** I am not worthy of success and recognition.

  AFFIRMATION: I deserve success, abundance, and recognition. I confidently step into my power and actively embrace the celebration of my achievements.

- **LIMITING BELIEF:** I am stuck in my current circumstances, and change is impossible.

  AFFIRMATION: I create my reality and can change my circumstances. I embrace change and welcome positive transformations in my life.

Consistency, belief, and conviction are the keys to harnessing the power of affirmations. It is crucial to repeat them consistently, especially when our limiting beliefs resurface. Doing so allows us to effectively rewire our subconscious mind and replace those limiting beliefs with empowering ones.

Many research studies have explored the psychological benefits of affirmations. One notable study conducted by Wood et al. in 2009 provides valuable insights into the impact of positive self-statements on performance and stress levels. This study's participants were assigned to solve challenging problems while facing stress-inducing scenarios.

The researchers divided the participants into three groups:

- The first group engaged in positive self-statements.

- The second group used neutral self-statements.

- The third group received no specific instructions regarding self-statements.

Throughout the task, the researchers closely monitored the participants' stress responses and performance levels to analyze the effects of the different self-statement approaches.

The study's results were remarkably compelling. Participants who engaged in the positive self-statement exercises performed significantly better on the key metrics than those in the neutral and control groups. These individuals also exhibited notably lower stress and anxiety levels during the challenging task. The findings suggested that practicing positive self-statements had a significantly positive impact on task performance and stress reduction.

This research supports the notion that positive affirmations can be valuable in challenging and reframing limiting beliefs. Gradually, consciously repeating positive statements that counteract negative beliefs shifts our mindset and self-perception. Over time, these affirmations can help build confidence, promote resilience, and enhance our overall well-being.

VISUALIZATION AND EMOTIONAL REHEARSAL

Visualization and emotional rehearsal are potent mental tools that can help reprogram and rewire our subconscious beliefs. By creating vivid, detailed mental images of successfully manifesting our deepest desires and carefully immersing ourselves in the associated positive emotions, we can send powerful new messages directly to our subconscious. This intentional mental process strengthens the neural connections that support and reinforce our new, more empowering beliefs over time.

The story of Jim Carrey, the renowned actor and comedian, magnificently shows the power of visualization, emotional rehearsal, and overcoming limiting beliefs. During the early 1980s, Carrey faced the challenges of breaking into the fiercely competitive entertainment industry. However, he used visualization techniques to manifest his dreams extraordinarily.

One notable aspect of Carrey's inspirational journey was his writing a personal check for $10 million, with the memo line stating, "for acting services rendered." He postdated it to 1995 and then carried that check in his wallet as a symbolic representation of the grand financial success that he was determined to achieve through the full realization of his acting talents.

In addition to the symbolic check, Carrey engaged in regular visualization practices. He would drive to Mulholland Drive in Los Angeles, gaze out over the city, and immerse himself mentally in the vibrant image of being a successful and highly sought-after actor. He skillfully crafted vivid scenarios in his mind, envisioning himself as the preeminent star in Hollywood, with a continuous flow of exciting work opportunities and directors and producers clamoring to collaborate with him.

During these visualization sessions, Carrey didn't just imagine his success, he lived it. He immersed himself in the vivid positive emotions associated with achieving his most ambitious goals. He allowed himself to deeply experience profound joy, exhilaration, and heartfelt gratitude as if he had already reached the pinnacle of success he passionately desired. Carrey firmly believed that by consistently visualizing his grandest dreams in meticulous detail and then wholeheartedly embodying the intensely positive emotions linked to their ultimate fulfillment, he would engrave a deep and motivating subconscious imprint that would propel him closer toward realizing those goals powerfully.

Eventually, the unwavering dedication Carrey displayed in his visualization and emotional rehearsal practices bore fruit. Just before the Thanksgiving holiday in 1995, Carrey received the extraordinary news that he had successfully secured the coveted leading acting role in the blockbuster comedy film *Dumb and Dumber*. Astonishingly, the compensation for this role amounted to precisely $10 million, aligning perfectly with the symbolic amount on the check he had written years earlier.

Carrey's remarkable story is a testament to the efficacy of visualization, emotional rehearsal, and transcending limiting beliefs. His stubborn belief in his abilities, combined with his unwavering commitment to visualizing his desired outcomes and wholeheartedly embodying the associated emotions, played a pivotal role in manifesting his dreams and catalyzing a transformative shift in his life.

ENERGY HEALING MODALITIES: EFT AND NLP

Energy healing modalities like Emotional Freedom Techniques (EFT) and Neuro-Linguistic Programming (NLP) offer additional tools to release subconscious limiting beliefs. In EFT, individuals actively tap specific meridian points while focusing on the limiting belief or emotion, restoring balance to the body's energy system. Research has investigated the effectiveness of EFT in different contexts. For instance, Church et al.'s 2013 study focused on veterans with PTSD. They conducted a randomized controlled trial, assigning participants to either an EFT or standard care group. The EFT group received six one-hour sessions, while the standard care group received no intervention. The study found that the EFT group experienced significant reductions in PTSD symptoms, including anxiety and depression, compared to the standard care group. These improvements were sustained at a three-month follow-up, suggesting long-term benefits.

Another study conducted by Waite and Holder in 2003 examined the effects of EFT on public speaking anxiety. The researchers randomly assigned college students with self-reported anxiety to either an EFT group or a waitlist control group. The EFT group received a one-hour session addressing their public speaking anxiety. The study showed that the EFT group experienced a significant reduction in anxiety levels and improved performance in public speaking tasks compared to the control group. These findings show EFT can effectively reduce public speaking anxiety and enhance performance in such situations.

On the other hand, NLP utilizes language patterns and techniques to reframe beliefs and emotions, leading to a shift in perception and the development of empowering beliefs. Although ongoing research continues to explore NLP's effectiveness, case studies have highlighted its potential in addressing deep-seated beliefs and emotions.

Wake et al.'s 2015 study examined the effectiveness of NLP interventions in reducing depression symptoms. Researchers randomly assigned participants diagnosed with clinical depression to either an NLP treatment group or a control group. The NLP group received a series of tailored NLP-based therapeutic interventions, whereas the control group did not receive any specific treatment. The study found that the NLP group demonstrated significant reductions in depressive symptoms compared to the control group, with these notable improvements in mental health outcomes sustained and maintained at a three-month follow-up assessment.

Similarly, Carrington and Colligan's 2011 study focused on the effectiveness of NLP in reducing public speaking anxiety. Researchers randomly assigned participants who reported a fear of public speaking to either an NLP or waitlist control group. The NLP group received NLP interventions targeting public speaking anxiety. The study showed that the NLP group experienced significantly reduced anxiety levels and increased self-perceived competence in public speaking tasks compared to the control group. These findings suggest that NLP interventions can be beneficial for lowering public speaking anxiety and enhancing self-confidence in such situations.

Overcoming subconscious limiting beliefs necessitates self-reflection, cultivating awareness, and employing various strategies. By actively challenging and reframing our beliefs, engaging in positive affirmations, using visualization and emotional rehearsal, and exploring energy healing modalities such as EFT and NLP, we can effectively release these constraints and manifest our aspirations. Scientific research and case studies provide compelling evidence for the effectiveness of these techniques, illustrating the brain's inherent capacity for change and the positive influence they can wield over our well-being and overall success. Equipped with these empowering tools, we can liberate ourselves from the shackles of subconscious limitations and construct a reality brimming with abundance and fulfillment.

"The pessimist sees difficulty in every opportunity.
The optimist sees opportunity in every difficulty."

WINSTON CHURCHILL

CHAPTER 5

Step 3:

CULTIVATE A POSITIVE MINDSET

AN OLD CHEROKEE chief sits under the soothing shade of a towering oak tree. His weathered eyes sparkle with wisdom as he imparts a profound lesson to his young grandson. The air crackles with anticipation as the boy leans in, his entire being focused on absorbing and embracing the timeless teachings of his revered elder.

With a deep, resonant voice that echoes the depths of his soul, the chief begins, "Listen closely, my son, for within me rages a battle of epic proportions—between two fierce primal adversaries locked in an endless, unrelenting conflict. One wolf embodies human nature's darkest, most destructive aspects, an evil force fueled by anger, envy, sorrow, regret, and insatiable greed. This wolf revels in arrogance, self-pity, guilt, resentment, and feelings of inferiority. This wolf is a master of deception, constantly weaving an intricate web of lies, false pride, superiority, and an over-inflated, ravenous ego."

The young boy's eyes widen, captivated by the intensity of the chief's words. He can sense the weight of the impending conflict.

"But, my grandson," the chief continues, his voice tinged with determination, "there is another wolf, a noble and radiant creature. It embodies all that is good within us. It is brimming with joy, peace, love, hope, and serenity. Humility courses through its veins, and every action is guided by kindness, benevolence, empathy, generosity, and truth. This wolf possesses an unwavering faith in the inherent goodness of the world. It is a beacon of light in the darkest times, a source of boundless compassion for all beings."

The young boy's heart quickens with anticipation as he gazes at his grandfather, his eyes pleading for an answer. He knows the answer to his question is the key to his inner battle. "But which wolf will emerge victorious, Grandfather? Which will stand triumphant?"

The old chief's gaze meets his grandson's, filled with ancient wisdom and unwavering conviction. "The one you feed," he declares, his voice a thunderclap in the wilderness. This simple yet profound statement echoes in the young boy's mind, leaving an indelible mark.

This Native American parable, *The Two Wolves*, has been retold countless times, captivating audiences across generations. The story is a potent reminder that we can choose how we perceive and respond to the world. It teaches us that our thoughts and emotions resemble wolves, persistently vying for our attention and influence over our actions.

By consciously nourishing the "good wolf" within us—through cultivating positive thoughts, emotions, and beliefs—we can experience a life brimming with peace, love, and fulfillment. Conversely, if we continuously feed the "evil wolf" by indulging in negativity, anger, and fear, we perpetuate a cycle of suffering and unhappiness.

The Two Wolves urge us to remain mindful of our thoughts and emotions and consciously select those that align with our values and aspirations. It reminds us that our mindset possesses the power to shape our reality and ultimately determine the quality of our lives.

THE PATHWAY TO OUR DEEPEST DESIRES LIES IN HONORING THE PROFOUND TRUTH THAT WE WIELD THE POWER TO SCULPT OUR REALITY THROUGH OUR PERCEPTUAL CHOICES.

Scientific studies have provided valuable insights into the benefits of maintaining a positive mindset in various aspects of life. In 2005, Seligman et al. conducted a comprehensive review of positive psychology interventions to assess their effectiveness and impact on well-being, life satisfaction, and overall mental health.

The review included studies investigating interventions such as gratitude exercises, positive self-reflection, strengths-based approaches, and mindfulness practices. These interventions actively aimed to cultivate positive emotions, enhance positive thinking patterns, and promote psychological well-being.

The review's findings were highly encouraging. They demonstrate that positive psychology interventions can significantly improve well-being, life satisfaction, and overall mental health. The interventions positively impacted individuals across different age groups and diverse populations.

One key finding was that positive psychology interventions effectively enhanced subjective well-being. Participants who engaged in these interventions reported higher positive emotions, such as joy, gratitude, and contentment. They also experienced a greater sense of life satisfaction and overall happiness.

The review revealed that positive psychology interventions positively influenced mental health outcomes. Participants who underwent these interventions showed reduced symptoms of depression, anxiety, and stress. They also exhibited improved resilience and adaptive coping strategies when faced with challenging situations.

Notably, the review highlighted the long-lasting effects of positive psychology interventions. Participants' well-being and mental health sustained positive changes over time, demonstrating the potential for enduring positive transformation through these interventions.

The review also sheds light on the underlying mechanisms through which positive psychology interventions exert their effects. These interventions promoted positive cognitive processes, such as optimistic thinking, self-compassion, and cultivating positive self-identities. They also facilitated the development of positive social connections and supportive relationships, which further contributed to improved well-being and mental health outcomes.

A 2012 meta-analysis by Boehm and Kubzansky explored the relationship between a positive mindset and cardiovascular health. The meta-analysis examined studies investigating the impact of positive psychological factors on cardiovascular health outcomes.

The meta-analysis revealed that individuals with a more positive mindset had a reduced risk of developing heart disease. Researchers also observed that those who maintained a positive outlook and emotional well-being exhibited lower rates of hypertension, a significant risk factor for cardiovascular problems.

The meta-analysis revealed that individuals with a positive mindset have a lower likelihood of experiencing adverse cardiovascular events, such as heart attacks or strokes. Positive emotional states linked to a positive attitude, including optimism, resilience, and happiness, may serve as protective factors against the onset and progression of cardiovascular diseases.

The analysis also showed that individuals with a positive mindset exhibited healthier lifestyle behaviors. They were likelier to engage in regular physical activity, adopt a balanced diet, maintain a healthy body weight, and not smoke. These lifestyle factors significantly influence cardiovascular health outcomes and contribute to a reduced risk of heart disease.

Lastly, the meta-analysis found that individuals with a positive mindset had increased life expectancy. The optimistic and resilient attitudes associated with a positive mindset may contribute to better overall health, enhanced stress management, and improved coping mechanisms, all of which can positively impact longevity.

ADOPTING A POSITIVE MINDSET HAS BEEN LINKED TO BETTER CARDIOVASCULAR HEALTH OUTCOMES, INCLUDING A LOWER RISK OF DEVELOPING HEART DISEASE AND LONGER LIFE EXPECTANCY.

In 2017, Moskowitz et al. conducted a randomized controlled trial to explore how a positive affect intervention affects individuals newly diagnosed with HIV—the intervention aimed to enhance positive emotions and foster a positive mindset. The study assessed the impact of this intervention on psychological well-being, coping abilities, and immune system functioning.

The trial demonstrated substantial improvements in psychological well-being among participants in the positive affect intervention group. They reported lower levels of depression, anxiety, and stress, showing an improvement in their overall mental health. The intervention positively impacted their emotional state and helped them develop more positive and adaptive coping strategies.

Furthermore, the positive affect intervention positively affected participants' coping abilities. They demonstrated increased resilience and a more remarkable ability to manage stressors associated with their HIV diagnosis effectively. This finding suggests that fostering a positive mindset through the intervention enabled them to face challenges more effectively and develop healthier coping mechanisms.

The trial also assessed the impact of the positive affect intervention on immune system functioning. The results showed improvements in immune system markers, including increased CD4 cell counts and improved immune response. These findings suggest that the positive affect intervention may have positively influenced the participants' immune system functioning, potentially contributing to their overall health and well-being.

In 2006, Otake et al. conducted a study that explored the impact of a "counting kindnesses" intervention on happiness levels. The intervention involved engaging in acts of kindness and reflecting on them.

The study found that participants who engaged in the "counting kindnesses" intervention experienced a significant increase in their happiness levels compared to a control group. Engaging in kind acts and reflecting on them fostered positive emotions and greater well-being.

Scientific studies have consistently demonstrated the benefits of maintaining a positive mindset. Research has shown positive psychology interventions enhance subjective well-being, improve mental health outcomes, and foster resilience and adaptive coping strategies. Maintaining a positive attitude has also been associated with improving cardiovascular health, promoting healthier lifestyle behaviors, increasing life expectancy, and positively affecting immune system functioning.

THE ROLE OF POSITIVITY IN MANIFESTATION

Cultivating a positive mindset is a transformative practice that can significantly impact our overall well-being and the outcomes we attract into our lives. As we wholeheartedly embrace positivity, we unlock many possibilities and establish a solid groundwork for personal growth and success.

> CONSCIOUSLY CHOOSING POSITIVITY AND RAISING OUR ENERGETIC VIBRATION, WE CREATE A HARMONIOUS RESONANCE WITH OUR DESIRED EXPERIENCES.

- **VIBRATIONAL ALIGNMENT**

  Positive thoughts, emotions, and experiences resonate at a higher frequency, while negative ones vibrate at a lower frequency. The goal is consciously aligning our vibration with positive manifestations by cultivating an optimistic mindset. This concept operates on the premise of "like attracts like"—by elevating our frequency through positive focus, we actively draw more positive outcomes into our lives. Adherents of this principle believe maintaining high-vibration states empowers us to harness the energetic Universe and create the circumstances we genuinely desire.

- **ATTRACT WHAT YOU FOCUS ON**

Our attention and intention play a crucial role in manifesting our reality. By consciously focusing on cultivating gratitude, abundance, and success, we are more likely to attract similar positive experiences into our lives. Consistently and intentionally aligning our thoughts and energy with our desired outcomes creates a powerful magnet for manifesting those positive realities. This principle underscores the importance of actively choosing our thoughts and consciously directing our attention toward what we wish to attract.

- **EMOTION AS A MANIFESTATION MAGNET**

Emotions are powerful magnets for attracting desired outcomes. Positive emotions such as joy, love, and gratitude are believed to have a higher vibrational frequency and can act as potent attractors for positive experiences. When we maintain a positive emotional state, we enhance the effectiveness of manifesting our desires. By cultivating positive emotions and consciously focusing on what brings us joy and gratitude, we align our energy with the experiences we wish to manifest, amplifying their likelihood of coming into our lives.

- **BELIEF AND EXPECTATION**

  Belief and expectation play a crucial role in manifestation. When we sincerely believe that positive results are within our reach and confidently expect them to occur, we align ourselves with the energy of those desired outcomes. This energetic alignment enhances our motivation, perseverance, and ability to recognize and act on opportunities that match our optimistic expectations. Regularly reinforcing these beliefs and expectations reinforces the neural pathways that support their actualization. Over time, this becomes a self-reinforcing cycle, propelling us ever closer to realizing our hopes and dreams.

- **RESILIENCE AND PERSISTENCE**

  Positivity contributes to resilience and persistence in pursuing our goals. A positive mindset allows us to maintain optimism, overcome obstacles, and keep going despite setbacks. It fosters a belief in our abilities and a sense of empowerment, allowing us to bounce back from challenges and continue moving forward. Positivity provides the emotional strength and mental fortitude needed to persevere through difficulties, adapt to change, and maintain focus on long-term goals. By cultivating resilience and persistence, we increase our chances of success and create a positive momentum that propels us toward our desired outcomes.

It is essential to acknowledge that while manifestation is controversial, many individuals find value in cultivating a positive mindset. A positive mindset promotes emotional well-being, motivation, and a proactive approach to achieving personal goals.

PRACTICAL EXERCISES AND TECHNIQUES FOR CULTIVATING A POSITIVE MINDSET

Having understood the significance of positivity in manifestation, it's time to explore practical ways to harness its power. Nurturing a positive mindset requires consistent dedication and applying diverse tools and techniques.

■ POSITIVE AFFIRMATIONS

Affirmations are powerful tools that can transform your thoughts and beliefs, leading to a more positive outlook. You are consciously rewiring your mindset by repeating affirmations that resonate with you. Incorporating positive affirmations into your daily routine helps reinforce empowering beliefs, boost self-confidence, and attract positive experiences.

- I choose to focus on the good in every situation.
- I am filled with gratitude for the blessings in my life.
- I trust in my ability to overcome any challenge.
- My thoughts and words create my reality.
- I am resilient and capable of handling whatever comes my way.
- I radiate positivity and attract uplifting experiences.
- I see the potential in myself and others.
- I am open to new opportunities and possibilities.
- I cultivate inner peace and emotional well-being.
- I am the architect of my happiness.

▪ VISUALIZATION

Visualization is a powerful technique that creates vivid mental images of your desired outcomes or situations. By visualizing yourself achieving your goals or experiencing positive events, you activate your imagination and align your mindset with what you want to attract into your life. Visualization enhances your focus, motivation, and belief in the possibility of your desired outcomes, making them feel more attainable. It is a powerful tool for manifesting your dreams and reinforcing a positive mindset.

– ABUNDANCE VISUALIZATION

Sit or lie comfortably, close your eyes, and take a few deep breaths. Imagine being surrounded by abundant positive energy, prosperity, and opportunities. Visualize yourself experiencing financial abundance, receiving unexpected windfalls, or steadily growing your bank account. Feel the emotions of gratitude, joy, and contentment as you imagine this abundance in your life. Spend a few minutes immersed in this visualization, allowing the positive feelings to permeate.

– CONFIDENCE VISUALIZATION

Picture yourself standing tall, shoulders back, and radiating confidence. Visualize yourself delivering a powerful presentation, acing an interview, or successfully navigating a challenging situation. See yourself speaking with clarity, conviction, and self-assurance. Imagine the admiring looks and positive feedback you receive from others as you walk into the room or interact. Feel the sense of pride and self-belief coursing through your veins. Reinforce this image of your confident, capable self.

> ENGAGE ALL YOUR SENSES—
> SIGHT, SOUND, SMELL, TOUCH,
> AND EVEN TASTE, IF APPLICABLE.

– HEALING VISUALIZATION

Imagine a warm, soothing light enveloping any areas of your body that need healing or restoration. Visualize this light, dissolving any physical, emotional, or mental blockages or discomfort. See your body and mind becoming rejuvenated, refreshed, and vibrant. Imagine your energy levels increasing, your mood lifting, and your overall well-being improving. Focus on the sensations of healing and wholeness throughout your being.

– PEACEFUL SANCTUARY VISUALIZATION

Imagine a tranquil, serene place that brings you a deep sense of calm and relaxation. It could be a beautiful beach, a lush forest, or a cozy, comforting space. Vividly picture the sights, sounds, and sensations of this peaceful sanctuary. Immerse yourself in the calming atmosphere, allowing your mind and body to find solace and rejuvenation. Spend time soaking in the peacefulness and let it permeate your entire being.

Through practice, visualization can help shift your perspective, cultivate an abundance mindset, and empower you to take concrete actions toward your aspirations. When you vividly imagine optimistic scenarios and desired outcomes, you send powerful signals to your subconscious. This reinforces your beliefs, aligns your thoughts and emotions with your goals, and helps you recognize and act on the opportunities that align with your visualized reality. Visualization taps into the connection between the mind and the body, allowing you to experience the physical sensations of your desired states, which can boost your motivation and self-confidence. Consistent visualization practice trains your brain to focus on what's possible rather than dwelling on obstacles and inspires you to take purposeful steps toward making your dreams a reality. The transformative power of visualization lies in its ability to reshape your perspective, cultivate a positive mindset, and guide you toward the life you wish to create.

> BY IMMERSING YOURSELF IN EMPOWERING MENTAL IMAGES, YOU CAN SHIFT YOUR MINDSET FROM SCARCITY AND LIMITATION TO POSSIBILITY AND ABUNDANCE.

- **MINDFULNESS AND MEDITATION**

Mindfulness and meditation practices effectively cultivate present-moment awareness, reduce stress, and foster a positive mindset. By setting aside dedicated time each day to practice mindfulness or meditation, you create space for inner calm and self-reflection. These practices quiet the mind, increase self-awareness, and allow you to observe your thoughts and emotions without judgment. As you develop mindfulness and meditation as habits, you become better equipped to respond to challenges with clarity, cultivate a positive outlook, and nurture a sense of inner peace.

– MINDFUL BREATHING

Find a comfortable seated or lying down position. Close your eyes and bring your attention to your breath. Observe the natural flow of your inhalations and exhalations without trying to control them. If your mind wanders, gently bring your focus back to your breath. Spend 5-10 minutes practicing this simple yet powerful mindful breathing exercise.

– PRESENT MOMENT AWARENESS

Find a quiet, comfortable place to sit or stand. Take a few deep breaths to center yourself. Shift your attention to your immediate surroundings, taking in the sights, sounds, smells, and sensations you are experiencing in the present moment. Notice the details without judgment - the colors, textures, movements, and ambient noises. Whenever your mind wanders, gently bring your focus back to the here and now. Spend 5-10 minutes practicing this grounding exercise, allowing yourself to be fully immersed in the current experience. Over time, you can expand this practice to carry with you throughout your daily activities, cultivating a greater sense of mindful presence.

- **BODY SCAN MEDITATION**

Lie down or sit in a comfortable, quiet space free from distractions. Get in a position that allows you to be relaxed yet alert. Close your eyes and bring your attention to the sensations in your body, starting from your toes and slowly working your way up. Notice any areas of tension, discomfort, or relaxation without judgment. Consciously relax each body part as you scan upwards, releasing any held stress or tightness. Breathe deeply and allow the tension to melt away. Finish by feeling your entire body in a state of calm and ease, fully present in the moment.

- **LOVING-KINDNESS MEDITATION**

Sit comfortably and close your eyes. Begin by cultivating feelings of compassion and kindness toward yourself. Repeat phrases like "May I be happy, healthy, and at peace." Expand this compassion to a loved one, a neutral person, and finally, all beings. Visualize sending waves of kindness and well-wishes to the entire world. End by feeling your heart filled with unconditional love and acceptance.

By incorporating these mindfulness and meditation practices into your daily routine, you can experience a quieter mind, reduced stress, and a more positive, present-moment awareness. These practices have the potential to profoundly impact your mindset and overall well-being, making them a valuable addition to your self-care routine.

- **SURROUND YOURSELF WITH POSITIVITY**

  The individuals, information, and media you surround yourself with are vital in shaping your mindset. You create an environment that fosters a positive attitude by deliberately seeking positive influences, such as supportive and optimistic individuals, uplifting books, inspirational quotes, or motivational podcasts. Pursuing relationships and connections that uplift and inspire you while consciously limiting your exposure to negativity, including negative news or toxic relationships, is essential. By making these choices, you establish a nourishing and uplifting atmosphere that supports your personal growth and cultivates a positive mindset.

- **SELF-CARE AND WELL-BEING**

  Taking care of your physical and emotional well-being is essential for cultivating a positive mindset. Engaging in activities that bring you joy, prioritizing self-care practices like regular exercise, nourishing your body with healthy food, and ensuring sufficient sleep all contribute to your overall well-being. Feeling good physically positively influences your mental and emotional state, making it easier to maintain a positive mindset. Remember to listen to your body's needs, practice self-compassion, and make self-care a priority in your daily life.

Remember that cultivating a positive mindset is an ongoing process that requires patience and consistency. Experiment with these exercises and techniques to find what works best for you and incorporate them into your daily routine. Over time, you can develop a positive mindset that attracts positivity and enhances your well-being.

HOW TO OVERCOME NEGATIVITY AND SELF-SABOTAGE

Negativity and self-sabotage can impede personal growth and hinder the manifestation of desired outcomes. However, effective strategies exist to overcome these challenges and cultivate a positive and empowering mindset. By implementing strategies consistently, you can break free from negativity and self-sabotaging patterns, paving the way for success and fulfillment.

1. **SELF-AWARENESS**

   Self-awareness is a crucial first step in breaking free from negativity and self-sabotaging patterns. By developing a deep understanding of your thoughts, emotions, and habitual behaviors, you create the foundation for lasting change. When you closely observe your inner experience, you can identify the negative thought loops, limiting beliefs, and self-destructive tendencies that hold you back. This self-observation allows you to pause before automatically reacting and consider more constructive responses. With practice, you'll grow increasingly adept at catching yourself when spiraling into unhelpful mindsets and redirecting your focus to more positive, productive perspectives. Self-awareness is the gateway to personal transformation—it gives you the power to interrupt ingrained negativity and replace it with an empowering, growth-oriented mindset.

2. **CHALLENGE AND REFRAME NEGATIVE PATTERNS**

   After cultivating self-awareness, the next crucial step is actively challenging and reframing negative patterns. By questioning the validity and accuracy of negative thoughts and beliefs, you can examine the evidence supporting them and consider alternative perspectives. This process of conscious reframing helps shift your mindset towards optimism, self-belief, and resilience in facing challenges. Instead of automatically accepting self-limiting beliefs, you can consciously choose more supportive and constructive thoughts that empower you to move forward. Challenging and reframing negative patterns is a powerful tool for breaking free from negativity and self-sabotage.

3. **CREATE A POSITIVE AND SUPPORTIVE ENVIRONMENT**

Building a positive and supportive environment is crucial for maintaining a positive mindset and overcoming negativity. Surround yourself with uplifting and encouraging individuals who believe in your potential and inspire you to grow. Engage in activities and hobbies that bring joy, fulfillment, and a sense of accomplishment. By fostering an environment that nurtures positivity and counters self-sabotaging tendencies, you create a space that supports your aspirations and helps you thrive. When you immerse yourself in an uplifting ecosystem, it becomes easier to cultivate and sustain a positive, empowered mindset.

4. **SET CLEAR AND ACHIEVABLE GOALS**

Setting clear and achievable goals helps to cultivate a positive mindset and overcome negativity. Break down larger goals into smaller, manageable steps to prevent being overwhelmed, increase motivation, and make consistent progress. Celebrate small victories along the way to reinforce positive behaviors and build momentum toward your desired outcomes. By setting realistic expectations and continuously moving forward, you cultivate a sense of purpose, accomplishment, and optimism, fueling your positive mindset. Goal-setting provides a structured framework for growth and helps you stay focused and motivated in the face of challenges.

5. PRACTICE SELF-CARE

Prioritizing self-care is vital for maintaining a positive mindset and overcoming negativity. Take care of your physical, emotional, and mental well-being to provide a solid foundation for positivity. Engage in activities promoting relaxation, such as regular exercise, meditation, or time in nature, to reduce stress, increase self-awareness, and boost positivity. Nurture yourself through healthy habits, adequate rest, and self-compassion to recharge, stay balanced, and approach life positively. When prioritizing your well-being, you're better equipped to navigate life's challenges with resilience and a constructive mindset.

6. SEEK PROFESSIONAL HELP AND GUIDANCE

In some cases, seeking professional help or guidance is necessary if you are struggling with deep-seated negativity and self-sabotaging patterns. Therapists, coaches, or mentors can provide valuable insights, tools, and support to navigate these challenges. They offer a safe space for you to explore underlying issues, develop strategies for personal growth, and address any psychological barriers that hinder a positive mindset. Professional guidance can provide a structured framework for self-reflection, development, and transformation, empowering you to overcome obstacles and cultivate lasting positivity. Reaching out for expert support can be a game-changer in your journey to break free from negativity and self-sabotage.

It is important to remember that overcoming negativity and self-sabotage is a journey that requires patience, perseverance, and self-compassion. Be easy on yourself. By consistently implementing these strategies and remaining committed to personal growth, you can break free from self-limiting patterns and create a more positive and rewarding life.

*"Gratitude can transform common days into Thanksgivings,
turn routine jobs into joy,
and change ordinary opportunities into blessings."*

WILLIAM ARTHUR WARD

Step 4:

PRACTICE GRATITUDE

F ROM A YOUNG age, my father introduced me to the captivating world of minerals, gems, and fossils. We would often visit the San Diego Mineral and Gem Society Museum, where we would be captivated by the sheer majesty of nature's artistic creations. Occasionally, he allowed me to choose a specimen to take home, sparking a lifelong fascination with these magnificent treasures.

In those early years, my father refrained from delving into the metaphysical intricacies surrounding crystals, perhaps believing that my young mind would struggle to comprehend such concepts. Instead, he imparted simple wisdom: "Choose the one that calls out to you." I can still picture him holding a crystal in his hand as if he possessed the ability to sense and listen to its silent voice. With conviction, he emphasized, "The one that feels right is the one you truly need."

Following his intuitive advice, I carefully chose my crystals, relying on the invisible connection that drew me to each specimen. Whether I sought love, peace, guidance, protection, or abundance, I selected them during times of need or lack. Over three decades, my collection expanded, occupying every available shelf space in my home.

As someone who incorporates gratitude into my daily routine, I regularly express appreciation for the items in my home. One day, as I expressed gratitude for each crystal in my collection, a profound realization washed over me. Unbeknownst to me, these stones were symbolic representations of the challenges I had overcome, becoming more than mere decorative pieces. And with every heartfelt expression of gratitude, I honored and acknowledged their role in my journey, day after day.

When we practice gratitude, our entire perspective transforms. It propels us to focus on the positive aspects of life, flooding the present moment with happiness and contentment. Gratitude can turn challenges into resounding victories, obstacles into promising opportunities, setbacks into incredible comebacks, and struggles into unwavering strengths. It goes beyond surface connections, delving deep to forge unbreakable bonds with others while fostering resilience and fortitude within us. Ultimately, gratitude becomes the key that unlocks a life of unparalleled joy and fulfillment.

Its transformative nature is akin to the crystals in my collection, each symbolizing a hardship beautifully transmuted into a source of deep appreciation. Gratitude allows us to view challenges as opportunities for growth rather than lingering scars from the past. It becomes the lens through which we perceive the breathtaking beauty and countless blessings embedded within every experience, no matter how arduous.

Through the embrace of gratitude, we cultivate a genuine appreciation for the entirety of our journey—the invaluable lessons learned and the precious moments cherished. It permeates every human experience, offering solace, tranquility, and overwhelming joy. It enables us to discover boundless fulfillment in the simplest of blessings surrounding us, propelling us toward a life overflowing with gratitude and abundant prosperity.

Neuroscientific research provides valuable insights into the effects of gratitude on brain function. In a 2016 study, Kini et al. investigated the impact of gratitude intervention on brain activity.

The researchers divided the participants into two groups:

- The first group engaged in gratitude intervention, which involved writing letters expressing gratitude to individuals who had positively influenced their lives.

- The second group received no specific instructions regarding gratitude-related activities.

The researchers used functional magnetic resonance imaging (fMRI) to measure brain activity in the participants. The fMRI scans focused on the medial prefrontal cortex, a brain region associated with reward processing and decision-making. The goal was to examine whether expressing gratitude would activate neural circuits involved in experiencing positive emotions and evaluating rewards. The study results showed that the gratitude intervention group exhibited increased activity in the medial prefrontal cortex compared to the control group. This finding suggests that expressing gratitude can activate brain regions associated with the experience of positive emotions and the evaluation of rewards. The study provides neuro-scientific evidence that appreciation positively impacts neural processes related to well-being.

> EXPRESSING GRATITUDE ACTIVATES PARTS OF THE BRAIN ASSOCIATED WITH POSITIVE EMOTIONS AND REWARDS, PROVIDING NEUROSCIENTIFIC EVIDENCE THAT GRATITUDE HAS TANGIBLE BENEFITS FOR OUR OVERALL WELL-BEING AND BRAIN FUNCTION.

Zahn et al. conducted a study in 2009 exploring the neural mechanisms underlying gratitude. The study aimed to investigate the brain regions associated with the experience of gratitude and its potential effects on social cognition and empathy.

During the study, researchers asked participants to think about significant people in their lives for whom they felt grateful while undergoing fMRI scans. The researchers focused on the anterior cingulate cortex and the medial prefrontal cortex, brain regions that play a role in social cognition and empathy.

The study's findings revealed that gratitude was associated with increased activation in the anterior cingulate and medial prefrontal cortex. These brain regions involve social cognition processes, such as perspective-taking, empathy, and understanding others' emotions. The activation of these areas during experiences of gratitude suggests that gratitude may enhance social interactions and promote empathic responses.

In a longitudinal study conducted by Ding et al. in 2015, the researchers investigated the effects of a gratitude intervention on brain structure. The study aimed to examine whether practicing gratitude through a journaling exercise could lead to structural changes in the brain.

The researchers divided the participants into two groups:

- The first group engaged in gratitude intervention, which involved journaling for several weeks and writing things they were grateful for.

- The second group received no specific instructions regarding gratitude-related activities.

To measure changes in brain structure over time, the researchers employed structural magnetic resonance imaging (MRI). They focused on the medial prefrontal cortex and the anterior cingulate cortex, brain regions associated with social cognition, emotion regulation, and empathy.

The study's findings revealed that the gratitude intervention group exhibited increased gray matter volume in the medial prefrontal cortex and the anterior cingulate cortex compared to the control group. These structural changes in the brain suggest that practicing gratitude through journaling exercises may have lasting effects on brain plasticity and function.

Collectively, these studies provide valuable insights into the neural mechanisms underlying gratitude and its effects on brain activity and structure. Expressing gratitude activates brain regions associated with positive emotions and reward processing, enhances social cognition and empathy, and can lead to structural changes in the brain. These findings highlight the potential benefits of cultivating gratitude for psychological well-being and social functioning.

GRATITUDE PRACTICES

Gratitude holds immense power as it influences our ability to manifest positive experiences. By embracing gratitude practices, we can shift our mindset, attract positivity, and enhance our manifestation abilities. Genuine expressions of gratitude emit a positive, high-frequency energy that aligns with our desired experiences, acting as a magnetic force for attracting favorable circumstances.

Developing a gratitude practice involves incorporating daily rituals and habits that cultivate appreciation. By understanding how gratitude amplifies the manifestation process and implementing these practices, we can establish a consistent gratitude routine that enhances our overall well-being and outlook.

▪ GRATITUDE JOURNAL

Maintaining a gratitude journal involves dedicating a few minutes daily to write things you are grateful for. By doing so, you create a tangible record of the blessings and joys that surround you. This simple act of acknowledging and appreciating the positive aspects of your life profoundly affects your perspective. As you consistently express gratitude for big and small things, you develop a sense of contentment and fulfillment. Writing your gratitude allows you to reflect on the abundance in your life, shifting your focus away from negativity and cultivating a greater appreciation for the present moment.

▪ MORNING REFLECTION

Taking a few moments each morning to reflect on what you are grateful for sets a positive tone for the day ahead. This early focus on gratitude helps frame your mindset and encourages daily appreciation and abundance. By consciously directing your attention towards the positive aspects of your life, you start the day with a sense of gratitude and optimism. Additionally, expressing appreciation to others is an effective habit. Whether through a simple verbal expression, a handwritten note, or a heartfelt message, acknowledging and appreciating others not only cultivates gratitude within yourself but also strengthens your relationships and fosters a sense of interconnectedness.

▪ MINDFUL PRESENCE

Practicing mindful presence involves fully engaging in the present moment and savoring the experiences you encounter. By slowing down and paying attention to the details of your surroundings, you develop a greater appreciation for the simple joys of life. Engaging your senses—taking notice of the beauty in nature, relishing the taste of your meals, cherishing the warmth of a smile or the laughter of loved ones—enhances your gratitude and connection to the world around you. Mindful presence allows you to shift your focus away from worries and distractions, fully immersing yourself in each moment's richness.

- **DAILY WALK**

Taking a daily walk to focus on what you are grateful for in your environment is a powerful practice. As you move through your surroundings, you intentionally direct your attention to the beauty of nature, the architecture of buildings, or the sights and sounds of your neighborhood. This intentional focus enhances your appreciation and develops a more profound gratitude for the world around you. Walking with gratitude allows you to find joy in the simplicity of your surroundings and cultivate a greater sense of connection to the present moment.

- **EVENING REFLECTION**

Taking a few moments each evening to reflect on the day and identify three things we are grateful for helps us end the day positively and reinforces the habit of gratitude. By intentionally recalling moments of joy, accomplishments, acts of kindness, or lessons learned from challenges, we focus on the positive aspects of our day. This practice helps us cultivate a sense of closure, release any lingering negativity, and reinforce the habit of gratitude, carrying that mindset into the next day.

- **ACTS OF KINDNESS**

  Engaging in acts of kindness and service toward others benefits them and cultivates gratitude within yourself. Volunteering, helping a friend, or performing random acts of kindness deepens your appreciation for humanity's interconnectedness and reinforces a sense of gratitude. By extending compassion and support to others, you recognize your ability to make a positive impact and develop a greater understanding of gratitude for the opportunities to contribute to the well-being of others.

Incorporating daily rituals and habits into your life creates a fertile ground for gratitude to flourish and permeate every aspect of your being. By journaling, starting the day with morning reflection, expressing appreciation, practicing mindful presence, going on gratitude walks, engaging in evening reflection, and performing acts of kindness, you develop a consistent and intentional gratitude practice that enhances your overall well-being and outlook on life. These practices help you shift your focus towards the positive, foster a greater appreciation, and cultivate a gratitude mindset throughout your life.

"The starting point of all achievement is desire."

NAPOLEON HILL

Step 5:

CLARIFY YOUR DESIRES

IT WAS UNMISTAKABLE. A large, ominous shadow loomed over the apartment building next to me, its piercing gaze fixated on my vulnerable form. With a shiver racing down my spine, I hastily flicked off the light switch, yanked the curtains shut, and dove under the covers, seeking solace from the lurking terror outside my window.

"MOOOOOMMMMMMMMMM!" I cried out, my voice trembling with fear. "He's out there again! Hurry, come quick!"

"That's what happens when you don't go to bed on time," my mother's voice resonated as she stepped into the room and closed the door behind her. "It's late, and tomorrow is a school day."

Akrouk was his name. He was a towering giant said to prey upon children who defied the bedtime rule, or so my mom said. He embodied my deepest fears, a creature whose presence was meant to coax me into slumber.

I whimpered and patted the space beside me, Mom's designated spot. "I waited for you," I murmured, my voice laced with relief and anticipation.

Mom nestled beneath the covers without hesitation, and I flung myself upon her, wrapping her tightly. This was our nightly ritual. As my guardian, she would strive to lull me to sleep as swiftly as possible, shielding me from the clutches of Akrouk.

With her voice guiding me, I would venture on extraordinary journeys to far-off lands and mystical realms. The perils that lurked outside my window faded insignificance as her storytelling's magic enveloped me. Each spoken word transformed my room into a vivid landscape of colors inhabited by fantastical creatures and fearless heroes. Mom wove tales handed down through generations, sharing timeless wisdom and life lessons from her youth. But her creativity knew no bounds. She spun tales of her invention, conjuring scenes that burst with life in my imagination. These stories ignited my lifelong passion for the power of storytelling. And as the last words of each tale gently dissipated into the air, I would surrender to slumber, cradled by the warmth of Mom's love and the enchantment woven into those cherished bedtime stories.

In a small Khmer village," Mom began, carrying me away to foreign lands, "there lived a wise, weathered old woman renowned for her wisdom. People from far and wide sought her counsel, seeking guidance on mundane and extraordinary matters. On one fateful day, a young man, plagued by uncertainty, approached her, his eyes brimming with questions. The old woman welcomed him warmly, sensing his troubled spirit, and invited him to sit by her side under the shade of a towering banyan tree.

'Wise one, I am adrift in a sea of desires, unsure of the path to follow. How can I find clarity?' the young man inquired.

With a knowing smile, the wise old woman bestowed upon him a small pouch. 'Within this pouch,' she whispered, 'lies a handful of seeds. Plant them in the four corners of your garden.'

Dutifully, the young man took the seeds and followed her instructions, tending to them with unwavering care. To his amazement, each corner of his garden burgeoned with life. In one corner, the seeds sprouted into a beautiful jasmine shrub adorned with aromatic blooms. A large and fruitful mango tree grew in another corner, providing plentiful nutrition. A bed of fragrant herbs like lemongrass, basil, and galangal flourished in the third corner, offering healing and culinary delights. Finally, a magnificent banyan tree emerged in the fourth corner, reaching toward the sky with unwavering strength.

Returning to the wise old woman, the young man sought further enlightenment. 'What do these seeds and their growth signify?' he inquired, his eyes ablaze with curiosity.

With a smile, the wise old woman responded, 'Each seed mirrors a desire within your heart. The jasmine embodies love and connection. The mango tree beckons abundance and prosperity. The herbs offer health and well-being. The banyan tree promises resilience and personal growth. As you tend to these desires, nurturing them with intention, attention, and action, you shall witness their unique qualities and potential. Embrace the beauty and abundance they offer, allowing them to guide you towards a life of fruition and meaning.'

The young man listened intently, absorbing the wisdom of the old woman's words. He thanked her and left, carrying the seeds and her teachings in his heart.

He tended to his desires with great care, watering them with dedication and nurturing them with perseverance. The jasmine bloomed, filling his life with love and meaningful connections. The mango tree bore fruit, ushering in prosperity and abundance. The herbs nurtured his body and soul, promoting well-being and vitality. The banyan tree's roots grew deep, offering strength and resilience in the face of challenges.

As the young man's garden thrived, so did his life. He found clarity and purpose, guided by the desires he had nurtured. Each day, he embraced the beauty and abundance his nurtured desires had brought him. And he walked a path of personal growth, supported by the resilience and strength of the banyan tree."

Mom's voice grew softer as she reached the end of the tale. "And so, the young man discovered that by tending to his desires and nurturing them with care, he created a life filled with love, prosperity, well-being, and personal growth. And he lived happily ever after."

I sighed contentedly, my eyelids growing heavy with sleep. Mom smiled and planted a gentle kiss on my forehead. "Sleep tight, my child," she whispered.

THE KEY TO CREATING A LIFE OF PROFOUND SIGNIFICANCE LIES IN OUR CAREFUL ATTENTION TO OUR MOST CHERISHED DREAMS AND AMBITIONS.

Clarifying your desires plays a crucial role in the process of manifestation. When you clearly understand what you truly desire, focusing your energy and intention toward bringing those desires into reality becomes easier.

- **JOURNAL WRITING**

  Set aside time to write freely about your hopes, dreams, and aspirations in a journal. Explore what truly matters to you without censoring or judging your thoughts and feelings. Let the words flow organically to uncover your heart's deepest desires.

- **VISUALIZATION EXERCISES**

  Close your eyes and vividly imagine your ideal life in as much detail as possible. Envision the specifics of your dream career, fulfilling relationships, desired lifestyle, and other essential elements. Allow your mind to wander freely, tuning into the emotions and sensations that arise as you picture your aspirations coming to life.

- **VALUES REFLECTION**

  Identify your core values—the principles, qualities, and beliefs that are most important to you. Contemplate how you can align your desires with what matters most, ensuring your aspirations are in harmony with your sense of purpose and integrity.

- **DESIRE MAPPING**

  Create a visual map or collage that represents your deepest desires. Use images, words, symbols, and other creative elements to capture the essence of what you long for. This tactile process can help crystallize your aspirations in a powerful, holistic way.

- **GUIDED INQUIRY**

  Ask yourself profound questions that prompt deeper self-reflection, such as "If I could do anything without limitations, what would I choose?" or "What legacy do I want to leave behind?" Allow intuition to guide your responses rather than defaulting to logical or socially conditioned answers.

- **DISCUSS WITH TRUSTED FRIENDS**

  Talk through your aspirations and uncertainties with loved ones who know you well. Allow their insightful perspectives and supportive presence to deepen your self-understanding. The act of voicing your desires out loud can also solidify and clarify them.

- **EXPLORE YOUR INTERESTS**

  Consider the activities, topics, and experiences that captivate and energize you. What do you find yourself consistently drawn to, even if it's "just a hobby"? Examining your genuine interests can point to underlying desires waiting to be cultivated.

- **IDENTIFY LIMITING BELIEFS**

  Explore any fears, doubts, or preconceptions keeping you from fully embracing your heart's true longings. Challenge these limiting beliefs with self-compassion and open-mindedness, creating space for your authentic desires to emerge.

The overarching purpose of these diverse exercises is to engage in a sustained, compassionate process of self-inquiry. This process empowers you to uncover your most authentic, deeply felt desires— rather than surface-level wants or socially conditioned expectations. With this clarity, you can thoughtfully align your life's direction and daily choices with what matters most to your heart and soul.

Beyond simply clarifying your desires, the true power lies in honoring and integrating them into your everyday life. When you uncover and embody your authentic longings, you invite the Universe to conspire in your favor. This awakens your innate ability to shape reality and create a life of deep fulfillment. The journey of desire clarification becomes an empowering act of self-discovery, self-trust, and self-actualization.

"The value of an idea lies in the using of it."

THOMAS EDISON

CHAPTER 8

Step 6:

SET CLEAR INTENTIONS

THOMAS EDISON, THE renowned and prolific inventor, is widely celebrated for his unwavering determination to create a practical and commercially viable electric light bulb. His story is a testament to the power of intention and the ability to persevere in the face of adversity.

Edison's laboratory became a haven of relentless experimentation, where he and his team fearlessly delved into the depths of possibility. Each failure was not a setback but a precious opportunity for growth, propelling them closer to the breakthrough they sought. With curiosity as their guide, they made incremental progress, refining their understanding with each new experiment.

Amidst skepticism and doubt from others, Edison remained steadfast. He recognized that failure was an integral part of the creative process, viewing each setback as a channel toward ultimate success. His famous words, "I have not failed. I've just found 10,000 ways that won't work," testify to his unwavering belief in his vision, fueling his persistence even in the face of uncertainty's darkest moments.

After years of tireless effort, Edison's perseverance paid off. He triumphantly developed a long-lasting, practical incandescent light bulb that forever altered the course of human history. As light permeated homes, streets, and once-darkened spaces, society transformed permanently. The electric light bulb became an enduring symbol of progress and innovation.

Today, we bask in the realization of Edison's vision in our everyday lives. Electric lighting has seamlessly integrated into modern society, empowering us to work, study, and engage in various activities irrespective of the time of day. It has opened new realms of possibility, enhancing safety and productivity and fundamentally reshaping our interaction with the world around us.

Edison's remarkable achievement is a potent reminder that intention, perseverance, and unwavering faith in one's vision can lead to extraordinary breakthroughs. His story inspires us to embrace failure as a catalyst for growth, persist in the face of challenges, and remain resolute in our goals, even amidst the arduousness of the journey. As we navigate our paths, we find solace and inspiration in Edison's enduring legacy. By setting clear intentions, learning from the invaluable lessons found within failures, and tenaciously pursuing our visions, we can manifest our dreams and impact the world, just as Edison did with the invention of the electric light bulb.

Scientific research further reinforces the profound efficacy of setting clear intentions in the manifestation process. A study conducted by Gollwitzer and Sheeran in 2006 sheds light on the impact of setting implementation intentions on goal achievement. The findings reveal that individuals who cultivate specific implementation intentions, meticulously planning the precise details of when, where, and how they will take action toward their goals, exhibit a significantly higher likelihood of successfully attaining their desired outcomes than those who do not engage in this practice.

The study's revelations underscore the importance of setting clear intentions that delineate actionable steps. Doing so, we construct a well-defined roadmap leading us toward our aspirations. Rather than merely expressing abstract desires, such as "I wish to lose weight" or "I aspire to start a business," setting implementation intentions involves meticulously outlining the concrete actions that will propel us toward these goals. For instance, an implementation intention for weight loss might manifest as "I will dedicate 30 minutes each morning to jogging at the nearby park."

This specificity and strategic planning level significantly bolster our capacity for attaining goals. With a clear plan, we are more likely to remain steadfast in our intentions and actively pursue the necessary actions to bring our desired outcomes to fruition. The detailed nature of implementation intentions enables us to surmount potential obstacles, providing us with a sense of direction and focus.

Setting implementation intentions activates our cognitive faculties, amplifying our motivation and dedication to our goals. Measuringly planning the specific actions required for goal achievement stimulates our brain's prefrontal cortex, the seat of decision-making, planning, and goal-directed behavior. This stimulation enhances our ability to stay on course, resist distractions, and overcome the challenges that may arise during our journey.

Furthermore, implementation intentions operate by forging connections between environmental cues and specific actions. We create mental associations between these cues and the desired behaviors by establishing a clear plan of when, where, and how we will take action. For instance, if you intend to cultivate a daily meditation practice, specifying that you will meditate every morning in a designated corner of your home helps establish a potent link between your environment and the intended behavior. This association facilitates initiating the desired action when the cue arises.

The legacies of other historical figures further illuminate the immense power of setting clear intentions and aligning our efforts toward specific goals. The pioneering physicist and chemist Marie Curie resolutely intended to study radioactivity and its effects. Despite her initial struggles and the prevailing gender biases of her time, Curie's unwavering dedication to her vision led to groundbreaking discoveries of the elements polonium and radium, and she became the first woman to win a Nobel Prize. Her story exemplifies the transformative potential of setting clear intentions and persistently pursuing them.

Similarly, Nelson Mandela, the iconic anti-apartheid leader of South Africa, clearly intended to dismantle apartheid and promote equality and justice. With unwavering determination and resilience, he fought against racial segregation, both peacefully and through armed resistance. Mandela's story illustrates the transformative power of setting intentions in line with one's values and persistently working towards them, inspiring people globally to stand against oppression and strive for a more equitable world.

Then there's Amelia Earhart, a pioneering aviator and advocate for women's rights, who set a clear intention to push the boundaries of aviation and challenge gender norms. With her determination and courage, she became the first woman to fly solo across the Atlantic Ocean. Earhart's intention and groundbreaking achievements shattered stereotypes and inspired generations of women to pursue their dreams fearlessly. Her story highlights the importance of setting audacious goals and daring to defy limitations, leaving a lasting legacy as a trailblazer in aviation history.

Setting clear intentions can guide our lives, giving us focus, motivation, and a sense of purpose. By articulating our goals with clarity, we activate our subconscious mind, align our actions with our aspirations, and open ourselves up to opportunities and synchronicities that support our journey.

CAREER

— I intend to become a respected leader in my industry by obtaining a management position within the next three years and consistently delivering exceptional results.

- I intend to learn and grow in my profession by enrolling in relevant courses and attending industry conferences to gain new skills and knowledge.

- I intend to create a supportive and collaborative work environment where everyone can thrive and reach their full potential by implementing mentorship programs and fostering open communication.

HEALTH AND WELLNESS

- I intend to achieve and maintain optimal physical health by adopting a balanced diet and regular exercise. I aim to complete at least three weekly workouts and incorporate more fruits and vegetables into my meals.

- I intend to prioritize self-care and mental well-being by practicing mindfulness meditation for 15 minutes every morning and allocating one hour weekly for a self-care activity, such as reading a book or relaxing bath.

- I intend to inspire and guide others to achieve their health and wellness goals through coaching or teaching. I am enrolling in a certification program and organizing workshops in my community.

RELATIONSHIPS

- I intend to cultivate a loving and supportive romantic relationship that brings joy, growth, and mutual fulfillment by actively participating in relationship-building activities, such as regular date nights and open, honest communication.

- I intend to build strong and authentic connections with my family members by scheduling monthly family gatherings and engaging in meaningful conversations that deepen our bonds.

- I intend to cultivate a circle of loyal and uplifting friendships that provide companionship, shared experiences, and emotional support by organizing regular social events and actively reaching out to maintain connections.

ABUNDANCE

- I intend to manifest abundance in all areas of my life, including financial prosperity, opportunities, and experiences that bring me joy and fulfillment by consistently saving 20% of my income and exploring investment opportunities.

- I intend to develop a positive and abundant mindset, attracting abundance and prosperity through gratitude practices, daily affirmations, and visualization exercises.

- I intend to create multiple streams of income and financial stability within the next five years by starting a side business and diversifying my sources of revenue.

CREATIVE

- I intend to express my unique artistic voice through my creations, inspiring and touching the hearts of others by completing one new artwork or creative project each month and participating in local art exhibitions.

- I intend to collaborate with fellow artists to create innovative and impactful works that challenge conventional boundaries by actively seeking collaborative opportunities and attending networking events in the art community.

- I intend to use my artistic talent to raise awareness and evoke change on important social and environmental issues by partnering with nonprofit organizations and creating art installations that address these topics.

SPIRITUAL

- I intend to deepen my spiritual practice and connect with my higher self, gaining wisdom and insight along my spiritual journey by dedicating 20 minutes daily to meditation and journaling.

- I intend to cultivate inner peace and mindfulness through regular meditation and self-reflection, nurture a harmonious connection with the divine by attending silent retreats, and practice gratitude daily.

- I intend to explore and embrace different spiritual teachings and practices, expanding my spiritual understanding and embracing a path that resonates with my soul by attending workshops and reading books on various spiritual traditions.

Setting clear intentions in various areas of your life establishes a well-defined path toward desired outcomes. These intentions act as guiding lights, illuminating your journey through life's challenges and opportunities. By taking consistent and inspired action, you foster alignment with your authentic self, propelling you on a transformative path of growth, self-discovery, and meaningful transformation.

"The first step towards getting somewhere is to decide that you are not going to stay where you are."

J.P. MORGAN

Step 7:

VISUALIZE SUCCESS

VISUALIZATION IS A powerful tool that taps into the creative potential of our minds, transforming our dreams into tangible reality. By immersing ourselves in vivid mental images of achieving our goals and experiencing the associated emotions, we prime our subconscious minds to seek opportunities and resources that align with our vision.

Neuroimaging studies have shed light on visualization's impact on cognitive processes, providing valuable insights into the neurological mechanisms underlying visual imagery. One notable study by Kosslyn et al. in 2001 aimed to understand how mental imagery activates specific neural networks associated with perception and attention.

This study asked participants to engage in visualization tasks that involved mentally manipulating various objects, scenes, and spatial relationships. Using functional magnetic resonance imaging (fMRI), the researchers observed changes in brain activity during these visualization exercises. The study revealed that visual imagery significantly activated specific neural networks linked to perception and attention. Brain regions responsible for processing visual information, such as the occipital lobe, displayed heightened engagement during the visualization tasks. Additionally, areas associated with attention and working memory, such as the parietal and prefrontal cortices, exhibited increased activity.

These findings provide scientific proof supporting the impact of visualization on cognitive processes and neural activation. By engaging in visualization exercises, we tap into the brain's visual processing systems and activate the same neural networks involved in perceiving and attending to real-world stimuli. The outcome suggests that visualization creates a potent mental simulation that influences our subconscious, shaping our perceptions and behaviors. The outcome indicates that visualization creates a potent mental simulation that influences our subconscious mind and supports the rewiring of our beliefs, empowering us to manifest our desired realities.

In 2013, Guang Yue, an exercise psychologist, conducted a study highlighting the influence of mental rehearsal and visualization on physical abilities and preparedness for success. Yue's research explored the intricate relationship between the mind and body, particularly physical movement.

Yue divided the participants into three groups and assigned them different activities:

- The first group physically performed a finger exercise.

- The second group imagined performing the finger exercise.

- The control group did not engage in any specific activity.

The study's results were remarkable. Yue discovered that the group that mentally rehearsed the finger exercise exhibited muscle activation patterns that closely resembled those of the group that physically performed the exercise. This intriguing finding suggests that the brain cannot differentiate between real and imagined experiences when activating muscles.

The implications of this phenomenon are significant across various aspects of our lives, including sports, physical rehabilitation, and personal development. Our brains' ability to simulate and replicate physical actions through mental rehearsal opens up possibilities. By visualizing ourselves performing specific tasks or activities successfully, we prime our neural pathways and enhance our performance.

Through consistent visualization and mental practice, we can effectively rewire our brains, improving our skills, confidence, and overall performance. This process, known as neuroplasticity, refers to the brain's ability to reorganize and form new connections based on our experiences and thoughts.

Visualization can also help us overcome mental barriers and increase our chances of success. Mentally rehearsing challenging situations can build resilience, develop coping strategies, and reduce anxiety. Athletes, for example, often employ visualization techniques to prepare for competitions mentally, envisioning themselves executing their routines or strategies flawlessly. This mental rehearsal enhances their physical performance and boosts their confidence and focus.

> MENTAL REHEARSAL AND VISUALIZATION CAN SIGNIFICANTLY IMPROVE PHYSICAL ABILITIES AND PERFORMANCE BY ACTIVATING THE BRAIN IN A WAY THAT CANNOT DISTINGUISH BETWEEN REAL AND IMAGINED EXPERIENCES, ALLOWING US TO REWIRE OUR BRAINS EFFECTIVELY THROUGH CONSISTENT MENTAL PRACTICE.

The power of visualization is a remarkable tool used by visionaries throughout history to shape their achievements and influence the world. With his mastery of visualization techniques, Walt Disney employed this powerful practice to bring Disneyland to life. As he walked through the empty field in California, his mind transported him to a future where the theme park existed, allowing him to picture its layout, rides, and attractions.

From the iconic Sleeping Beauty Castle to the bustling Main Street, U.S.A., Walt meticulously mapped out every intricate detail in his mind's eye. These vivid mental images became the blueprint for the magical kingdom he sought to create. Walt's visualizations extended far beyond the physical aspects of Disneyland. He mentally simulated visitors' experience, envisioning the laughter, excitement, and joy filling the air. He imagined families strolling hand in hand, children's eyes wide with anticipation, and the enchantment that awaited them at every turn. These visualizations served as more than fleeting daydreams; they became the foundation for Disneyland.

As Walt continued to refine his vision, he encountered numerous challenges and skeptics whom he needed to convince of the feasibility of his ambitious project. However, his unwavering belief in the power of visualization propelled him forward. He used his visualizations to inspire himself and convey his vision to others, igniting their imagination and enlisting their support.

Walt's ability to articulate his visualizations with clarity and passion allowed him to assemble a team of talented individuals who shared his dream. From architects and engineers to artists and animators, each person was captivated by Walt's unwavering vision. Together, they worked tirelessly to bring the imagined world of Disneyland into reality.

Throughout the process, Walt Disney remained resolute in his commitment to preserving the essence of his visualizations. He insisted on maintaining the integrity of his original ideas, even when faced with budget constraints or technical limitations. His unwavering dedication to his vision ensured that Disneyland became an immersive and transformative experience for its visitors.

When Disneyland finally opened its gates to the public, Walt's visualizations became a tangible reality. The magic he had imagined in his mind had materialized into an enchanting realm that captivated the hearts of millions. Visitors immersed themselves in a world where stories unfolded, dreams came to life and witnessed the full glory of visualization firsthand.

Walt Disney's legacy as a master of visualization continues to inspire generations of dreamers and creators. His ability to harness the power of his imagination and transform it into a tangible reality serves as a testament to the potential within each of us. Walt's story reminds us that visualization is not merely a passive act of dreaming but a proactive practice that can shape our destinies and leave an indelible mark on the world.

Just as Walt Disney harnessed the power of visualization, other notable individuals have done the same to manifest their aspirations. The brilliant inventor Nikola Tesla could visualize his inventions with extraordinary detail. Tesla claimed to see his creations clearly in his mind's eye, down to the tiniest intricacies. He refined his designs through intense visualization and brought groundbreaking inventions that shaped the modern world. From alternating current (AC) electrical systems to wireless communication, Tesla's visualized visions paved the way for technological advancements that continue to impact our lives today.

Tesla's visualization process was a crucial aspect of his inventive genius. He would immerse himself in deep concentration, shutting out external distractions and focusing on the problem. With his eyes closed, he would mentally manipulate the components of his inventions, observing their behavior and interactions in his mind.

In Tesla's visualizations, he saw the flow of electricity, envisioning the intricate pathways it would take and how to harness it for practical applications. He would mentally experiment with various configurations, adjusting and refining his designs until they met his exacting standards. According to reports, Tesla himself claimed to have constructed entire machines in his mind before manifesting them physically.

This intense visualization practice allowed Tesla to overcome obstacles and challenges during the invention process. He would visualize potential setbacks, foresee potential flaws or limitations in his designs, and then work to address them in his mind before even beginning the physical construction. This approach saved him time and resources, as he could refine and optimize his inventions before ever building a prototype.

Tesla's ability to visualize his inventions in such vivid detail allowed him to communicate his ideas to others. He could clearly articulate complex concepts, using his visualizations as a guiding framework, which enabled him to collaborate effectively with engineers, investors, and other stakeholders, as he could convey his vision in a tangible and relatable manner.

Through his incredible power of visualization, Tesla revolutionized the world of electrical engineering. His innovations in AC power transmission and distribution laid the foundation for the electrification of cities, powering industries, and transforming how we live. Tesla extended his vision to wireless communication, envisioning a world where information could traverse great distances without physical wires.

Today, the impact of Tesla's visualized inventions is undeniable. Our modern electrical grid, the basis of our power infrastructure, relies on AC systems that Tesla pioneered. The wireless technologies we use daily, from smartphones to Wi-Fi, owe their existence to Tesla's visionary ideas.

Nikola Tesla's story demonstrates the power of visualization in unlocking human potential. His ability to see beyond the limitations of the present and visualize a future filled with innovative possibilities changed the trajectory of technological progress. Tesla's visualized visions inspire inventors, scientists, and dreamers, reminding us of the transformative power of imagination and visualization in shaping our world.

Even Albert Einstein, the renowned physicist, employed visualization techniques to aid his scientific breakthroughs. Einstein famously imagined himself riding a beam of light, a pivotal visualization in formulating his theory of relativity. By visualizing complex concepts, Einstein could grasp and manipulate them in his mind, leading to his revolutionary theories in physics.

Einstein's visualization process went beyond mere thought experiments; it involved immersing himself in imagined scenarios and experiencing them firsthand. In his mind, he would embark on imaginary journeys through space and time, observing the effects of different physical phenomena. By mentally placing himself in these situations, he could gain unique insights into the fundamental nature of the Universe.

For instance, the visualization of riding a beam of light allowed Einstein to explore the consequences of traveling at near-light speeds. As he envisioned this extraordinary imaginary journey, he contemplated the distortions of space and time that would occur, ultimately leading to his groundbreaking theory of special relativity. This powerful mental visualization became a guiding metaphor that helped him unravel the complex mysteries of time dilation, length contraction, and the equivalence of mass and energy.

Einstein's visualizations also extended to more abstract concepts. When developing his theory of general relativity, which describes the gravitational force as the curvature of spacetime, he employed visualizations of warped surfaces. By mentally picturing the bending and warping of a flexible sheet, he could grasp the intricate relationship between mass, energy, and gravity.

Moreover, Einstein did not confine his visualizations to his theoretical work. He often used mental imagery to aid his problem-solving process. When faced with complex mathematical equations, he would visualize geometric shapes, patterns, and physical analogies to guide his thinking. These visual representations helped him make intuitive connections and unlock new insights.

Einstein's visualization process was an integral part of his genius. It allowed him to transcend the limitations of traditional approaches and explore the frontiers of physics. He revolutionized our understanding of the Universe by combining his remarkable imagination with rigorous mathematical reasoning.

Furthermore, Einstein's visualizations were not limited to his solitary contemplation. He also used visual metaphors and thought experiments to communicate his ideas to others. Through vivid and relatable imagery, he could convey the essence of complex theories to a broader audience. This ability to visualize and articulate his concepts in accessible ways contributed to his widespread influence and enduring legacy.

Einstein's use of visualization highlights the power of imagination in scientific discovery. By creating mental representations of abstract concepts, he transcended the boundaries of conventional thinking and challenged established paradigms. His visualizations served as guides and catalysts for his intellectual pursuits, enabling him to perceive hidden relationships and uncover profound truths about the nature of reality.

Albert Einstein's story reminds us that visualization is not limited to art or personal goals. It has a vital place in scientific inquiry and problem-solving. By harnessing the power of imagination and visual thinking, we can expand our understanding, push the boundaries of knowledge, and make groundbreaking discoveries that shape the course of human progress.

These examples highlight the profound impact of visualization in manifesting goals, unlocking creativity, and pushing the boundaries of human potential. These visionaries transformed their aspirations into reality by harnessing the power of the mind's eye, leaving an indelible mark on the world. Their stories emphasize that visualization is not a mere daydreaming exercise but an intentional practice that aligns our thoughts, emotions, and actions in pursuit of our deepest desires. Whether achieving personal success, creating groundbreaking inventions, or unraveling the mysteries of the Universe, visualization serves as a catalyst that empowers us to tap into our innate potential and shape the reality we desire.

HOW TO VISUALIZE

Visualization is a powerful technique that allows us to tap into our minds' creative power and align our energy with our desired outcomes. By engaging in structured visualization, we can unlock the depths of our imagination and bring our dreams to life.

1. **SET THE STAGE**

    Find a quiet, comfortable space to relax and fully immerse yourself in the visualization process. Create an environment that supports a sense of tranquility and allows you to let go of distractions.

2. **CLARIFY YOUR DESIRES**

    Clearly define what you want to manifest through visualization. Be specific about your intentions and the outcomes you wish to experience. The more precise and detailed your desires, the more potent your visualization becomes.

3. RELAX AND CENTER YOURSELF

Take a few moments to calm your mind and relax your body. Deep breathing exercises, meditation, or gentle stretching can help you release tension and enter a state of relaxation. This state of calmness enhances your receptivity to the process.

4. VISUALIZE WITH INTENSITY

Close your eyes and visualize your desired outcomes with intensity and clarity. Use all your senses to make the visualization experience as vivid as possible. See the colors, hear the sounds, feel the sensations, and immerse yourself in the emotions associated with your desired manifestation.

5. ENGAGE YOUR EMOTIONS

Infuse your visualization with positive emotions such as joy, gratitude, excitement, and love. Feel the feelings as if your desires have already manifested. Emotionally connecting with your visualization amplifies its manifestation potential.

6. STAY OPEN AND RECEPTIVE

Let go of any doubts, limitations, or skepticism. Cultivate a mindset of openness and receptivity to the manifestation of your desires. Trust in the power of your visualization practice and believe in the possibilities that lie ahead.

7. PRACTICE CONSISTENTLY

Consistency is vital for visualization. Set aside dedicated time each day to engage in structured visualization exercises. By making it a regular practice, you reinforce your intentions and strengthen the energetic alignment with your desired outcomes.

For instance, if you aspire to become a successful writer, visualize yourself seated at your desk, surrounded by shelves overflowing with your own written works, the rhythmic sound of your fingers dancing on the keyboard, the aroma of freshly brewed coffee wafting through the air, and the deep sense of fulfillment that accompanies completing a manuscript. Allow the emotions of joy, gratitude, and satisfaction to wash over you as you fully surrender to the experience. Repeat this visualization exercise regularly to fortify your intentions and amplify your manifestation abilities.

Clarifying our desires and utilizing visualization is essential for manifesting them with clarity and purpose. When we align our thoughts and emotions with our goals, we unlock the limitless creative potential of the mind, activating the cosmic forces that work together to bring our dreams to life. By intentionally focusing on our visualizations, we empower ourselves to confidently explore infinite possibilities and create a life filled with abundance, joy, and deep fulfillment.

"Action is the foundational key to all success."

PABLO PICASSO

Step 8:

TAKE INSPIRED ACTION

MY ATTENTION WAS fixated on the boats nestled within the harbor. Their presence captivated me, and I couldn't help but be curious about their stories. The sign proudly proclaimed the name "Dana Point Harbor." A quick search on my phone revealed this harbor could accommodate approximately 2,500 boats, some of which serve as permanent residents. For some odd reason, an inexplicable yet undeniable sadness washed over me.

Having returned home to Southern California to be closer to my family, I have spent the past seven months leisurely traversing the shores of this picturesque coastal town. As I passed the stationary vessels, their dormant presence tugged at my heartstrings. It was evident that most of these boats had yet to venture beyond the harbor since my arrival. Perhaps it was a touch of whimsy or a poetic inclination, but I couldn't resist the urge to talk to them.

"I'm sorry you're confined here."

"I hope you have the chance to venture out soon."

"This is not your true purpose."

The ships that grace the harbor serve as a profound metaphor for the journey of our lives. Like those vessels, we are inclined to seek refuge within the familiar boundaries of our comfort zones, finding solace in the known and the predictable. While familiarity and predictability offer a sense of stability, we must recognize that our true purpose extends far beyond the sheltered harbor of our routines.

Our purpose lies in the courageous embrace of uncharted waters, in welcoming the unknown with open arms, and in setting sail toward the limitless horizons of possibility that we unlock the potential for our dreams and desires to manifest. By venturing beyond the safe confines, we set upon a transformative voyage where our aspirations can find fulfillment and our true selves emerge.

That is your true purpose.

While remaining anchored shields us from uncertainties and potential disappointments beyond, it also denies us the transformative power of expansion. Inspired action, like a gust of wind in our sails, propels us forward, urging us to unfurl our sails with unwavering determination. It pushes us to confront the turbulent waves of challenges, for overcoming these obstacles means we discover our inner strength and resilience and grow into the best versions of ourselves.

Venturing beyond the harbor opens us to abundant opportunities and experiences. We align ourselves with the boundless flow of the

Universe, allowing synchronicities to guide us toward our deepest desires. No matter how seemingly small, each step we take creates ripples that resonate with the radiant energy of manifestation.

Inspired action is the key to transforming our aspirations into tangible reality. While cultivating self-love, overcoming subconscious beliefs and resistance, practicing positivity and gratitude, setting clear intentions, and visualization are all important, it is through deliberate and purposeful action that we propel ourselves along the path of manifestation. It's crucial, however, to understand that not all actions are created equal, and we must discern between inspired action, which is driven by our innermost desires and values, and mere effort.

DISTINGUISH INSPIRED ACTION
FROM MERE EFFORT

Inspired action goes beyond mere exertion of effort. It stems from a deep sense of alignment with our intentions and desires, arising from a place of intuition and inner wisdom. When we allow a higher source to guide us, we tap into a powerful force that leads us toward our desired outcomes.

Cultivating inner clarity and connection is essential to aligning our actions with our intentions. Practices such as meditation, journaling, or time in nature can help us quiet the external noise and attune to our inner guidance. Doing so makes us more receptive to acting harmoniously with our genuine desires. Inspired action is not about going through the motions or following a prescribed set of steps. It involves co-creating with the Universe, consciously aligning our thoughts, emotions, and actions with our desired outcomes. This alignment creates a profound synergy that amplifies our ability to attract and manifest what we seek.

Taking inspired action also requires trust and surrender. It means letting go of the need to control every detail and allowing the Universe to work its magic. It requires being open to unexpected opportunities and embracing calculated risks. Stepping out of our comfort zones may be challenging, but genuine transformation occurs within these moments of expansion.

By discerning between inspired action and mere effort, we tap into a higher source of guidance and actively co-create with the Universe. Cultivating inner clarity, practicing trust and surrender, and embracing new possibilities unlock the transformative power of inspired action, allowing us to manifest our dreams into reality.

Scientific research provides additional evidence supporting the relationship between action and manifestation. A 2010 study by Aarts et al. focused on "priming" and its impact on goal-directed behavior. Priming involves activating specific mental constructs or behaviors through exposure to particular stimuli.

The authors conducted a series of experiments to explore the influence of priming individuals with action-related stimuli on their engagement in goal-directed behaviors. One experiment involved subliminally presenting participants with action-related or neutral words to prime them with an action-oriented or neutral mindset. Following the priming phase, participants were assigned tasks that required goal-directed behavior, such as completing specific puzzles or exercises.

The study's findings indicated individuals primed with action-related stimuli were likelier to engage in goal-directed behaviors than those not primed or primed with neutral stimuli. Action priming significantly impacted participants' motivation and willingness to pursue their goals.

EXPOSURE TO ACTION-ORIENTED CUES CAN ACTIVATE MENTAL CONSTRUCTS AND INCREASE MOTIVATION, LEADING TO GREATER GOAL PERSISTENCE.

Notably, the study demonstrated that the effects of priming on goal-directed behavior were not limited to immediate actions but could have a lasting impact. Participants primed with action-related stimuli exhibited higher persistence in pursuing their goals, even in subsequent tasks or situations.

These findings suggest that action-oriented cues have the potential to activate and facilitate goal pursuit. Exposure to stimuli associated with action or movement can influence mindset, motivation, and subsequent behavior, leading to increased engagement in goal-directed activities.

The study significantly contributes to the existing body of research, reinforcing the relationship between action and manifestation. It underscores the pivotal role of activating action-related mental constructs through priming in initiating and sustaining goal-directed behaviors. Researchers observed a measurable impact on participants' motivation and goal pursuit by priming individuals with action-oriented cues, such as action-related words or images.

These findings have profound practical implications in various domains, including personal development, goal setting, and behavior change. They suggest incorporating action-oriented cues or prompts in relevant contexts can significantly enhance individuals' motivation and commitment to achieving their goals. Actively priming individuals with stimuli related to action may influence their mindset and increase the likelihood of purposeful steps toward desired outcomes.

Taking inspired action, aligning our actions with our intentions, and distinguishing between effort and true alignment allows us to harness a potent creative force. We unlock the transformative power to manifest our desires by cultivating inner clarity, trust, and willingness to step outside our comfort zones. Scientific research reinforces the significance of action in goal-directed behavior, highlighting the crucial role of inspired action on our path to manifestation.

STRATEGIES FOR INSPIRED ACTION

When it comes to manifesting our dreams, taking inspired action is crucial. By adopting practical strategies and motivational insights, we empower ourselves to move forward and progress towards our desired outcomes.

- **SET CLEAR AND SPECIFIC GOALS**

  Setting clear and specific goals is essential to effectively integrate action into the manifestation process. By defining your desires and breaking them down into actionable steps, you provide yourself with clarity and direction. For example, if your goal is to improve your health and fitness, you can set specific objectives, such as exercising for 30 minutes each day or following a nutritious meal plan. Clear goals make it easier to identify the necessary actions to take.

- **CREATE A PLAN**

  Developing a plan that outlines the actions required to achieve your goals is essential. This roadmap helps you determine the milestones and timelines for your journey. By regularly assessing your progress, you can stay on track and adjust as needed. Your plan could involve creating a monthly schedule of tasks or setting deadlines for specific milestones along the way. Having a well-defined plan helps you stay organized and motivated.

- **TRUST YOUR INTUITION**

  Listening to your inner voice and following your instincts are crucial when deciding on your manifestation journey. Trusting your intuition guides you toward opportunities and choices that align with your desires. For instance, consider how you feel about each choice when considering career options and trust the path that resonates most with you. Your intuition can provide valuable insights and steer you toward the actions that will lead to the manifestation of your dreams.

- **STEP OUT OF YOUR COMFORT ZONE**

Embracing growth and taking calculated risks that push you beyond your comfort zone contributes to manifesting your dreams. Engaging in challenging activities that foster personal development is essential. Stepping out of your comfort zone may involve public speaking, trying new experiences, or undertaking projects that stretch your skills and abilities. Expanding capabilities and willingness to explore new opportunities open doors to personal and professional growth.

- **SEEK SUPPORT AND MENTORS**

Surrounding yourself with individuals who support your aspirations and can offer guidance and mentorship is invaluable. Learning from those who have already achieved what you desire can significantly accelerate your progress. Seek mentors, join communities, or engage with like-minded individuals who can provide encouragement and advice. A solid support system can help you stay motivated, gain valuable insights, and navigate challenges more effectively.

- **PRACTICE RESILIENCE AND PERSEVERANCE**

Setbacks and obstacles are standard on the path to manifestation, but cultivating resilience and perseverance enables you to overcome them. Understand that setbacks are a natural part of the process and view them as opportunities for growth and learning. Embrace challenges as a path toward your goals and maintain a resilient mindset. Practice perseverance by staying committed to your journey even when faced with difficulties.

- **CONSISTENT ACTION**

Taking small, consistent steps each day that align with your intentions is crucial. Regular action builds momentum and keeps you in the flow of manifestation. It is essential to maintain a consistent effort towards your goals, even on days when motivation may be lacking. Consistency is critical to making progress and nurturing the manifestation process. You reinforce your commitment and dedication to your dreams by consistently taking action.

Embracing inspired action and stepping outside the boundaries of our comfort zones presents us with a world of abundant possibilities and enriching experiences. By doing so, we establish a harmonious connection with the vast flow of the Universe, permitting the serendipitous alignment of events to lead us toward fulfilling our most profound aspirations. With every deliberate and purposeful step, we tap into the transformative force within us, ultimately transforming our dreams into tangible realities.

"Holding onto anger is like grasping a hot coal with the intent of throwing it at someone else; you are the one who gets burned."

GAUTAMA BUDDHA

Step 9:

FORGIVE

TEN YEARS HAD passed since my initial heartbreak, the pivotal event mentioned in the book's introduction that catalyzed my spiritual awakening. Now, fate had brought me to the brink of yet another shattering moment. It felt familiar, like déjà vu, but this time, the pain surpassed anything I had felt before. It plunged me into a cruel abyss, relentlessly piercing me with its intensity.

In the depths of my anguish, my ego reveled in the turmoil. It found solace in the confines of suffering, deriving a perverse satisfaction from the emotional storm of hurt, anger, sadness, disappointment, trauma, and distrust. In those dark moments, a haunting whisper of escape tempted me toward oblivion.

One day, overwhelmed by despair, I stood on the second story of a bustling mall. The world blurred around me as I teetered on the edge of a decision that could change everything. The thought of jumping, surrendering to the void, became alarmingly clear. In that harrowing moment, I questioned if the fall would end my pain.

But as I stood on the precipice, a glimmer of clarity cut through the despair. Realizing how my actions would devastate those around me stirred deep emotions. I saw their faces, scarred forever, flash before my eyes. It was a wake-up call, a reminder of the interconnectedness of our lives and the ripple effects of our choices. In that darkest hour, I chose to step back to face my pain with courage and vulnerability.

After the waves of torment and self-pity subsided, I undertook a humbling voyage of deep reflection. I used introspection to challenge my limiting beliefs and seek the root of my pain. In those moments, a revelation shifted my perspective entirely.

This process showed me how our tools and patterns shape our lives. It became clear that when others' actions cause our suffering, it's crucial to recognize that their behavior often stems from their pain and struggles—it's rarely about us. It's tempting to internalize their actions when hurt, believing we are at fault or unworthy. But we can free ourselves from this burden by cultivating understanding.

I grasped that their behavior reflected their difficulties and the battles they fought within themselves. This perspective allowed me to transcend personalization and view their actions with empathy and compassion. Recognizing that their behavior wasn't a deliberate act of harm towards me but an expression of their pain opened the door to forgiveness. This shift in perception created the potential for healing and growth for both myself and those who caused me pain.

Throughout history, spiritual leaders have taught the power of forgiveness. The Dalai Lama, a beacon of compassion, eloquently captured its essence, saying, "If you want others to be happy, practice compassion. If you want to be happy, practice compassion." Their wisdom reminds us that love and compassion, universal rules, break the cycle of suffering—not hatred and revenge. By extending forgiveness to ourselves and others, we traverse on a transformative pilgrimage, nurturing our shared humanity and embracing the worth within each soul.

We unlock ourselves when we realize that the ego often personalizes and clings to separateness. Our higher self, connected to a greater truth, understands the interwoven nature of our existence. It's through the conscious act of forgiveness that something extraordinary happens.

FORGIVENESS BREAKS THE CYCLE OF SUFFERING AND NURTURES OUR SHARED HUMANITY.

Through forgiveness, I transcended the pain that once held me captive, liberating myself from burdens that weighed heavily. Releasing resentment, I forged a resilient and renewed connection with the source of my suffering. In this realm that transcends the limitations of the ego, the barriers of separateness fade away, making room for unity, unconditional love, and interconnectedness to flourish.

Our essence lies beyond the ego's confines, where forgiveness flourishes and genuine connections thrive. By embracing forgiveness, we tap into the wellspring of our being, fostering unity and harmony with ourselves and others. This transformation is not a one-time event but a continuous process, requiring a willingness to relinquish the desire for revenge.

While this path presents challenges, the rewards are immeasurable. Forgiveness liberates us from the suffocating grip of victimhood, empowering us to reclaim our power and choose our responses to life's challenges. By releasing the burdens of the past, we fully embrace the present. Forgiveness catalyzes compassion, empathy, and understanding, nurturing inner peace and harmonious relationships.

I now see that my darkest moment held a concealed gift amidst the pain and despair. I discovered the key to self-liberation through forgiveness, paving the way for tremendous personal growth and transformation.

THE TRANSFORMATIVE POWER OF FORGIVENESS FOR MANIFESTATION

Forgiveness is a mystical force intricately entwined with manifestation, surpassing mere release. It catalyzes transformation, empowering us to shift our energy and align with our desires, ultimately manifesting a reality infused with positivity and abundance. Negativity, anger, resentment, and vengeful thoughts burden us, aligning with lack and hardship. However, when we embrace forgiveness and release these heavy emotions, our energy rises to higher realms of love, compassion, and gratitude. Within this elevated frequency, the magnetic pull of abundance draws near, ushering in opportunities, fulfillment, and wondrous experiences that ignite extraordinary possibilities within our manifestations.

▪ CLEAR EMOTIONAL BLOCKS

Forgiveness liberates us from the heavy emotional burdens that weigh us down. It allows us to release pent-up anger, resentment, and hurt, creating healing and growth space within our hearts and minds. By acknowledging and letting go of these emotions, we free ourselves from their grip, enabling us to move forward with renewed clarity, lightness, and emotional well-being.

▪ SHIFT PERSPECTIVES

Forgiveness opens the door to a profound shift in perspective. It empowers us to transcend the role of a victim and embrace our power. Rather than dwelling on past grievances, forgiveness enables us to see the lessons and growth opportunities hidden within painful experiences. It allows us to view challenges as catalysts for personal transformation, empowering us to rewrite our narratives and approach life with renewed optimism and resilience.

▪ CULTIVATE SELF-LOVE AND COMPASSION

Forgiveness is an act of self-love and compassion. By extending forgiveness to ourselves, we acknowledge our fallibility, embrace our imperfections, and grant ourselves permission to heal and grow. It involves treating ourselves with kindness, understanding, and acceptance and fostering a nurturing environment for personal development. Through self-forgiveness, we cultivate a deep sense of self-worth, compassionately attending to our needs and paving the way for self-empowerment and transformation.

BREAK LIMITING BELIEFS

Forgiveness shatters the chains of limiting beliefs that hold us back from realizing our potential. It challenges ingrained narratives of unworthiness, guilt, and self-doubt that we may have internalized. By forgiving ourselves and others, we recognize our inherent capacity for growth and change, dismantling the barriers that hinder our transformation. This newfound freedom from limiting beliefs allows us to embrace new possibilities, expand our horizons, and step into our authentic selves.

WHEN WE FORGIVE, WE DO NOT ERASE THE PAST, BUT REWRITE ITS MEANING - TRANSFORMING WOUNDS INTO WISDOM, AND ENEMIES INTO TEACHERS.

ALIGN WITH ABUNDANCE

Forgiveness aligns us with the energy of abundance. We raise our vibrational frequency by releasing negative emotions and letting go of grudges, creating a fertile ground for manifestation. Forgiveness enables us to cultivate gratitude, appreciation, and positivity, attracting abundance into our lives. As we align with the abundant nature of the Universe, we open ourselves to opportunities, synchronicities, and the fulfillment of our desires.

HARMONIZE RELATIONSHIPS

Forgiveness is a powerful tool for healing and harmonizing relationships. It allows us to let go of resentment, bitterness, and blame, paving the way for reconciliation and understanding. When we extend forgiveness to others, we create space for healthy communication, empathy, and compassion to flourish. By fostering an atmosphere of forgiveness, we can transform strained relationships, build deeper connections, and create a sense of harmony and unity.

ENHANCE SELF-REFLECTION AND GROWTH

Forgiveness provides a gateway for self-reflection and personal growth. It encourages us to examine our actions, motivations, and behavior patterns. Through forgiveness, we gain insights into our vulnerabilities and areas for improvement. This self-awareness becomes the foundation for personal growth as we make conscious choices to evolve, heal, and become the best versions of ourselves.

OPEN DOORS TO NEW POSSIBILITIES

When we release the grip of past grievances, we create space in our lives for fresh experiences, relationships, and opportunities to enter. By letting go of what no longer serves us, we invite the unknown and embrace the potential for positive change. Forgiveness opens us to unexpected paths, inspiring transformations we may have never envisioned.

- **AMPLIFY MANIFESTATION POWER**

  Forgiveness amplifies our manifestation power by aligning our intentions with positive energy. As we free ourselves from the negativity of resentment and grudges, we become clearer channels for manifesting our desires. Forgiveness enables us to focus our energy on what we truly want, harnessing the power of intention and aligning ourselves with the vibrations of abundance.

- **EMBRACE INNER PEACE**

  We create a space within ourselves for tranquility and harmony by releasing the emotional turmoil associated with past hurts. Forgiveness lets us release the need for revenge or retribution, replacing it with a calm acceptance. This inner peace becomes the foundation for personal transformation and manifestation, enabling us to navigate challenges gracefully and with poise.

By releasing the emotional burdens of the past, we align our energy with the frequencies of abundance, love, and self-empowerment. Forgiveness clears the way for new possibilities, strengthens our relationships, and cultivates the inner peace necessary for manifestation to flourish. As we embrace the transformative power of forgiveness, we become liberated from limiting beliefs, expand our perspectives, and connect to our deepest well of self-love and compassion. This alchemical process elevates our vibration, magnetizing the fulfillment of our desires and ushering in a reality infused with positivity, harmony, and the boundless gifts of the Universe. Forgiveness is not merely a cathartic release but a mystical force that cata-lyzes our capacity to manifest the life of our dreams.

> **FORGIVENESS IS THE KEY THAT UNLOCKS THE DOOR TO OUR MOST PROFOUND MANIFESTATIONS.**

HOW TO FORGIVE

Forgiveness is a transformative process that can heal emotional wounds, mend broken relationships, and liberate the human spirit. It involves finding the strength to forgive others who have caused us harm and extends to the power of self-forgiveness. This journey requires courage, introspection, and a willingness to let go of past pain. By embracing forgiveness, we can cultivate compassion, find healing, and ultimately experience the profound liberation that forgiveness brings. Through forgiveness, we free ourselves from resentment and open the door to personal growth and deeper connections.

1. **ACKNOWLEDGE AND VALIDATE YOUR EMOTIONS**

    Forgiveness begins with acknowledging and validating your emotions. Recognizing and accepting the pain, anger, or hurt you feel because of the offense is essential. Acknowledging these emotions allows you to experience them fully and authentically. This step is crucial because it will enable you to confront the offense's impact and honor your emotional well-being.

> ENGAGING IN INTROSPECTION AND SELF-ACCEPTANCE
> ARE CRUCIAL ELEMENTS OF FORGIVENESS.
> THEY ENABLE US TO HEAL, ACCEPT ACCOUNTABILITY,
> AND MOVE FORWARD WITH SELF-COMPASSION.

2. UNDERSTAND THE SITUATION AND GAIN PERSPECTIVE

To forgive, it's helpful to gain a deeper understanding of the situation and the factors that contributed to it. This involves putting yourself in the other person's shoes and trying to see things from their perspective. It doesn't mean condoning or excusing their actions but seeking empathy and recognizing that everyone has struggles and limitations. By gaining perspective, you open yourself to finding common ground or a shared humanity that can facilitate forgiveness.

3. RELEASE RESENTMENT AND LET GO

Letting go of resentment and negative emotions is a crucial aspect of forgiveness. Holding onto resentment only prolongs suffering and keeps you emotionally tethered to the past. Releasing these emotions is a conscious choice that frees you from their burden. Forgiveness doesn't mean forgetting or pretending the hurt didn't happen but choosing not to let it define your present and future. By creating space for healing and growth, you release resentment and move forward with a renewed sense of freedom and possibility. This liberates you from the weight of past grievances, opening the door to new beginnings.

4. PRACTICE EMPATHY AND COMPASSION

Forgiveness often involves cultivating empathy and compassion. It means extending understanding and compassion to the person who hurt you and recognizing their pain, struggles, and humanity. It doesn't mean justifying or excusing their actions but acknowledging that everyone makes mistakes and has vulnerabilities. Practicing empathy and compassion can help break down barriers and foster a sense of connection, which is crucial for forgiveness to flourish.

5. SELF-REFLECTION AND HEALING

Self-reflection is an essential part of the forgiveness process. Reflect on your thoughts, feelings, and reactions to the offense. Explore any patterns or triggers that may have contributed to the situation. Engage in healing practices that resonate with you, such as journaling, meditation, or seeking support from a therapist or counselor. Self-reflection allows you to gain insight into yourself, heal any wounds that may have been triggered, and take responsibility for your growth and well-being.

6. SET BOUNDARIES

Forgiveness doesn't mean that you must forget or condone the offense. Establishing and maintaining healthy boundaries is essential to protect yourself from further harm. Communicate your boundaries clearly and assertively, ensuring your needs and well-being are respected. Setting boundaries is an act of self-care and self-respect, allowing you to create a safe space for healing and growth while maintaining your emotional integrity.

7. PRACTICE SELF-FORGIVENESS

Extending forgiveness to yourself is crucial in the process of forgiveness. Recognize that you are human and capable of making mistakes. Forgive yourself for any perceived shortcomings or errors you may have made in the situation. Self-forgiveness is an act of self-compassion and acceptance. It allows you to let go of self-blame, learn from your experiences, and move forward with renewed self-love and growth.

8. GIVE IT TIME

Forgiveness is a journey that takes time and varies for everyone. It's essential to be patient with yourself and the process. Healing and forgiveness may not happen overnight, and that's okay. Allow yourself the necessary time and space to heal, process your emotions, and work through any lingering pain. Be gentle with yourself and trust that forgiveness will unfold naturally with time.

9. SEEK SUPPORT

Forgiveness can be challenging; seeking support from trusted friends, family members, or professionals can be invaluable. Share your thoughts and feelings with someone who can provide guidance, empathy, and a non-judgmental ear. Therapists, counselors, or support groups specializing in forgiveness can offer insights, tools, and emotional support throughout your forgiveness journey. Seeking support can provide additional perspectives, validation, and encouragement when the path to forgiveness is difficult.

It is essential to understand that forgiveness is not a one-time event but a continuous practice. It demands empathy, compassion, and the release of the desire for retribution. While it may be arduous, requiring time and effort, its rewards are immeasurable. Through forgiveness, we transcend limitations, liberating ourselves from the shackles of the past. This ongoing practice opens doors to a future brimming with possibilities, where the realization of our deepest desires awaits.

"*Let go, or be dragged.*"

ZEN PROVERB

Step 10:

SURRENDER AND TRUST

A SEVERE DROUGHT ravaged the village, casting a shadow of despair over the once-thriving community. The sun beat down relentlessly, baking the earth and leaving the fields barren and lifeless. Farmers watched helplessly as their crops withered away, their hopes fading like the dying plants.

Among them was a humble farmer known for his unwavering work ethic and resilience. While others succumbed to worry and desperation, he chose a different path. With unwavering faith in the Universe, he surrendered to the harsh reality and placed his trust in something more significant.

Amidst the arid landscape, the farmer took a deep, steadying breath and mustered the strength to sow the precious seeds for the next season's crop. His skeptical neighbors, filled with doubt and cynicism, questioned his actions and motives, scoffing at his audacious determination and unwavering belief in a favorable outcome.

But the farmer remained undeterred, a glimmer of quiet determination shining in his eyes. "I trust in the rhythms of the Universe," he calmly declared, his voice carrying unwavering conviction. "I have done my part to prepare the soil and plant the seeds, and now I surrender the outcome to forces greater than myself."

Days turned into weeks, and weeks into months. The village continued to suffer under the relentless grip of the drought. The other farmers, driven by fear and desperation, toiled tirelessly to revive their fields, their minds clouded by doubts and worries. They strained and labored, trying to force the land to yield a bountiful harvest, but their efforts were unsuccessful.

Meanwhile, the farmer who had surrendered to the Universe tended to his land confidently, with a tranquil acceptance of nature's rhythms. He nurtured the soil, caring for each seed with unwavering devotion. Though the odds were against him, he remained steadfast in his belief that there was a higher plan at work. While his neighbors grew increasingly anxious and disillusioned, this farmer moved gracefully, trusting that the Universe would provide in its own time.

And then, as if the heavens had heard his silent prayers, the sky darkened with gathering clouds. The long-awaited rain poured, casting a soothing spell over the parched earth. The village rejoiced as the life-giving drops quenched the land's thirst.

Magnificent transformations unfolded before the farmer's eyes as the drought finally broke. Where once there was desolation, a splendid field teeming with vibrant crops stood. The farmer's harvest was abundant, a testament to the power of surrender and trust.

The other farmers approached him in awe, their faces etched with wonder and curiosity. "How did you manage to defy the odds?" they asked, their voices tinged with admiration and envy.

With a smile, the farmer explained, "I surrendered my worries and trusted in the natural rhythms of life. I realized I could not control the weather or the outcome, but I could control my actions and attitude. By surrendering and trusting in the Universe, I allowed space for miracles to unfold."

The parable of *The Farmer's Luck* is a timeless reminder of the transformative power of surrender and unwavering faith. It teaches us that surrendering control and embracing trust in the Universe are vital yet often overlooked elements of the manifestation process. It entails letting go, releasing attachment to specific outcomes, and cultivating a profound trust in divine timing. By surrendering to the natural flow of life, you create space for greater ease, serenity, and alignment to enter your manifestation journey.

LET GO OF CONTROL

Just as electrical theory teaches us that a wire with less resistance allows for a seamless energy flow, surrendering control and releasing attachment are the catalysts that unlock the natural course of our desired outcomes.

Let me share the story of a friend who yearned for a fulfilling romantic relationship. He had a clear and detailed vision of his ideal partner, meticulously outlining her traits, qualities, and physical attributes. His criteria ranged from specific height and weight preferences to cultural background, beauty standards, and professional success. It seemed as though he was in search of a mythical unicorn.

However, despite his unwavering pursuit, he clung to this idealized notion and was unwilling to let go. This attachment created a rigid framework through which he evaluated potential relationships, often leading to disappointment and frustration. He dismissed opportunities that didn't perfectly align with his predetermined checklist, failing to see the potential in connections that could have developed into something beautiful.

His inability to release this narrow vision became a source of tension and anxiety, akin to grasping tightly onto something intangible. By clinging to his idealized image, he unintentionally closed himself off from the vast array of possibilities and potential partners beyond his self-imposed limitations.

After years of being single, he confronted the consequences of his attachment and recognized how it hindered his ability to connect with others and experience genuine love. In a moment of clarity and courage, he decided to release his predetermined criteria and abandon the tightly held image he had constructed. This surrender opened his heart to the unpredictable nature of love and allowed him to embrace the beauty of authentic connections, free from preconceived notions.

In this newfound state of openness, he discovered that love could transcend the limitations of his checklist. He met someone who, although not conforming to every specific detail he once deemed essential, possessed qualities and shared a deep connection that far surpassed his expectations.

Their love is a testament to the power of letting go and being receptive to life's unexpected gifts. He found something even rarer and more meaningful by releasing the idea of finding a unicorn.

UNDERSTANDING THAT WE CANNOT CONTROL EVERY ASPECT OF OUR LIVES IS FUNDAMENTAL TO MANIFESTING OUR DESIRES.

Just as electrical currents effortlessly traverse paths of least resistance, surrendering control and embracing trust align us with the natural energetic flow of manifestation. This alignment mirrors nature's grand symphony, where a tree bends gracefully with the wind rather than breaking, water carves through solid rock, lightning seeks conductive paths, and rivers shape their surroundings.

Letting go of control is a transformative practice that invites serendipity and unexpected marvels into our lives. By relinquishing rigid expectations and placing unwavering trust in the Universe's wisdom, we open ourselves to a world brimming with infinite possibilities. In this harmonious dance with the Universe, our desires find resonance, orchestrating events and connections that flawlessly align with our highest good.

> WHEN WE RELEASE OUR ATTACHMENTS AND WHOLEHEARTEDLY TRUST IN THE DIVINE TIMING AND WISDOM OF THE UNIVERSE, WE CREATE AN OPEN CHANNEL FOR OUR DESIRES TO MANIFEST.

RELINQUISH ATTACHMENT TO SPECIFIC OUTCOMES

Releasing attachment to specific outcomes is paramount to manifesting our desires. We often fail to recognize alternative paths that may lead to greater fulfillment when we fixate on a particular result. By surrendering our attachment and embracing an open-minded approach, we create a spaciousness that allows the Universe to surprise us with unexpected blessings.

I once had a client who sincerely desired to establish his mixed martial arts (MMA) clothing company. His vision was clear—to create stylish designs that deeply resonate with athletes and fans alike. Despite the fierce competition in the MMA apparel market, he was resolute in manifesting his dream precisely as he had envisioned.

As he continued his entrepreneurial journey, he encountered

numerous obstacles that tested his resilience. He grappled with the challenge of finding suppliers who met his stringent criteria for quality materials, faced financial constraints that strained his resources, and navigated the unforgiving landscape of the fashion and entertainment industry. The path to manifesting his desired outcome proved far more arduous than he had initially anticipated.

In the face of discouragement, he took a step back to reassess his approach. It dawned on him that his attachment to the specific outcome of building a wildly successful and renowned MMA clothing brand was limiting his perspective. He consciously released his attachment to a rigid business plan and remained open to new opportunities and adaptations.

Rather than fixating solely on traditional retail channels, he ventured into uncharted territory. He contemplated launching an online store, forging collaborations with local gyms and MMA events, and even sponsoring athletes who resonated with his brand's core values. Furthermore, he entertained the idea of creating a vibrant community around his brand, offering comprehensive training resources and organizing exhilarating MMA-related events.

In the process of relinquishing his attachment, he stumbled upon unexpected blessings. He forged connections with like-minded entrepreneurs in the MMA industry who shared his vision, garnering invaluable insights and unwavering support. Through the power of his online presence and active engagement within the community, he attracted a devoted following of customers and ardent MMA enthusiasts who deeply resonated with his brand and its designs.

As he wholeheartedly embraced the ebb and flow of his journey, he realized that his original vision of success was one possibility among many others. Gradually, he began to appreciate the intrinsic beauty of the process and the positive impact he could make, irrespective of the scale of his business. He fearlessly experimented with limited edition releases, collaborated closely with athletes to curate unique designs, and wholeheartedly incorporated feedback from athletes and customers into the iterative product development process.

And then, one fateful day, a major competitor within the MMA apparel industry noticed his brand's immeasurable value and untapped potential. Astounded by the unparalleled quality of his designs, they extended an offer to acquire his company for a substantial sum. This acquisition rewarded him with financial abundance and opened doors to broader distribution channels and expanded market reach.

> ADOPTING A FLEXIBLE MINDSET INVITES
> MANIFESTATION BEYOND OUR EXPECTATIONS.

When we let go of our attachment to specific outcomes and adopt a flexible mindset, we invite the manifestation of our desires in ways that exceed our initial expectations. The manifestation process becomes a collaborative dance, where we work hand in hand with the

Universe to shape our desires into realities that go beyond what we originally envisioned. By embracing the flow of our journey, appreciating the process, and remaining open to new possibilities, we create space for the Universe to surprise us with unexpected blessings and guide us towards paths that lead to even greater fulfillment and impact.

TRUST IN DIVINE TIMING

Trusting in divine timing is essential when surrendering and allowing the natural unfolding of the manifestation process. It involves having faith that everything happens at the perfect moment, even if it doesn't align with our initial expectations. By trusting in a greater plan for us in the Universe, we let go of impatience and cultivate peace and contentment in the present.

A dear friend of mine provides a real-life example of the power of trusting in divine timing. She strongly desired to relocate to a new city and embark on a fresh chapter in her life. Feeling stagnant in her current surroundings, she yearned for a vibrant community, a fulfilling career, and loving relationships. With great enthusiasm, she began searching for job opportunities and browsing real estate listings in her desired city.

However, despite her diligent efforts, she encountered numerous obstacles. Job applications went unanswered, and the housing market seemed fiercely competitive. Frustration and doubt started to creep in, casting doubt on the attainability of her dream. Sensing her growing unease, I advised her to surrender her attachment to specific timelines and outcomes.

Taking this advice to heart, she resolutely released her need for immediate results and embraced the process. Instead of relentlessly pushing against the challenges, she focused on finding inner peace and contentment in the present moment. She prioritized self-care, deepened her spiritual practice, and nurtured her existing meaningful relationships.

During this phase of surrender and trust, she remained open to unexpected opportunities. Attending networking events, participating in community gatherings, and connecting with like-minded individuals became her regular practice. Through these meaningful interactions, she fortuitously discovered an online part-time position perfectly aligned with her skills and interests. Though it wasn't the full-time job she initially sought, she recognized it as a path on her journey. Not only did it provide her with income, but it also allowed her to move to the city she had always desired.

She felt drawn to a local organization while surrendering and trusting the Universe. Intrigued by their mission and values, she wholeheartedly contributed her skills and efforts to their cause. Little did she know that this experience would be truly transformative. Through her active involvement, she had the privilege of meeting inspiring individuals who became her closest friends and introduced her to an incredible job opportunity that aligned perfectly with her long-term career aspirations.

With renewed confidence and trust, she fearlessly pursued the position. This time, her efforts flowed effortlessly, and she received an offer far exceeding her expectations. Overjoyed, she could finally embrace all she had envisioned. Surrounded by supportive colleagues and like-minded friends who shared her passions, she knew in her heart that she had found her place of belonging.

TRUSTING IN DIVINE TIMING EXTENDS BEYOND PERSONAL DESIRES AND MANIFESTATIONS. IT ACKNOWLEDGES THAT THE UNIVERSE OPERATES ON ITS TIMELINE, ORCHESTRATING EVENTS AND SYNCHRONICITIES BEYOND OUR LIMITED HUMAN UNDERSTANDING.

This remarkable journey is a powerful reminder of the beauty that unfolds when we surrender and trust the path. By cultivating trust, remaining open to new possibilities, and embracing the present moment, we manifest outcomes that align with our deepest desires and bring profound fulfillment. Surrender and trust enable us to co-create our reality, gracefully navigate challenges, and unlock infinite possibilities.

Trusting in divine timing requires us to release impatience and cultivate deep faith. It asks us to relinquish ego-driven desires for immediate results and embrace the unfolding of life's plan. In this surrender, we find peace and contentment, knowing that everything is happening as it should, even if it doesn't align with our preconceived notions.

By trusting in divine timing, we acknowledge the greater intelligence in the Universe and recognize that forces beyond our control guide us toward our highest good. It invites us to stay grounded and present in the moment, developing resilience and trust.

Trusting in divine timing is not passive observation but an active alignment of our intentions, thoughts, and actions with our desires while surrendering the need for immediate results. It is a delicate dance between inspired action and allowing the Universe to guide us toward optimal outcomes.

> TRUSTING IN DIVINE TIMING REQUIRES COURAGE, FAITH, AND AN UNWAVERING BELIEF IN THE INHERENT GOODNESS OF LIFE. EMBRACING THIS PRACTICE OPENS US TO THE MAGIC AND MIRACLES THAT OCCUR WHEN WE ALIGN WITH THE NATURAL FLOW OF EXISTENCE.

It also invites us to cultivate gratitude, appreciating the lessons and opportunities that come our way, even in the face of challenges or setbacks. We see the purpose behind every twist and turn, leading us closer to our authentic selves and fulfilling our soul's purpose.

As you venture into unfamiliar territory, remember to trust in life's divine timing. Surrender your need for control, embrace the present, and have faith that everything is unfolding as it should. Believe that the Universe has a plan for you, and the right people, opportunities, and experiences will come into your life at the perfect time.

REPETITION

*"We are what we repeatedly do.
Excellence, therefore, is not an act, but a habit."*

WILL DURANT

Step 11:

REPETITION

BRUCE LEE FAMOUSLY said, "I fear not the man who has practiced 10,000 kicks once, but I fear the man who has practiced one kick 10,000 times." It underscores the essence of expertise and effectiveness through dedicated repetition and refinement. By persistently repeating and perfecting a single task, one can attain elevated levels of skill and execution.

As mentioned in the introduction, you may feel déjà vu and notice a pattern of repetition while reading. The rhythmic cadence of these words is no accident. Instead, it is a deliberate technique, harnessing the power of repetition to reprogram your mind and unlock new pathways of possibility. Just as the mind readily absorbs information through focused study, this cyclical phrasing imprints fresh perspectives, allowing them to take root in your consciousness. It is a process of gentle yet steady transformation. Trust that this intentional pattern is your guide, calling you to let go of resistance and embrace the path of least effort.

Repetition holds immense significance across various domains. In music, musicians diligently practice scales, chords, and pieces to cultivate muscle memory, enhance technique and elevate their overall performance. Athletes rely on repetitive training to improve physical abilities, whether mastering specific movements in sports like basketball or soccer or perfecting intricate gymnastics routines. Repetition empowers athletes to execute complex actions instinctively, respond swiftly to challenges, and achieve consistent outcomes.

In education, repetition forms the bedrock of learning. Repeated exposure to information aids in consolidating knowledge and augmenting retention. Students review and practice study materials, engage in drills and exercises, and undergo multiple assessments to reinforce their understanding and mastery of subjects. Repetition strengthens neural connections, facilitating easier recall and practical application of acquired knowledge.

The creative process also thrives on repetition. Artists, writers, and inventors embark on iterative journeys, repeatedly refining their work by revisiting their drafts, experimenting with different styles, and persistently iterating on ideas to align their creations with their envisioned outcomes.

Like learning a dance move, repetition is essential for these concepts to become ingrained in your very being. So, embrace repetition as a vital building block for your mental reprogramming. It is fundamental in life's grand tapestry, particularly in manifestation. By consistently repeating positive thoughts, beliefs, and actions, we align our subconscious with our intentions and aspirations, harmonizing the symphony of our inner and outer worlds.

Practices such as affirmations and visualization are powerful tools to imprint new beliefs and thought patterns into our subconscious. By engaging in these repetitive endeavors, we overwrite any preexisting negative or limiting beliefs that may hinder our progress in manifesting our genuine desires.

The power of repetition is remarkable. It can transcend the ordinary and usher in the extraordinary. It serves as a catalyst, propelling individuals on a transformative odyssey from learners to leaders and from students to teachers. Mastery is not a destination reached through solitary endeavor but a profound transcendence attained through the harmonious rhythm of repeated iterations.

> EMBRACING REPETITION ALLOWS NEW BELIEFS AND PATTERNS TO SINK DEEPLY INTO OUR CONSCIOUSNESS, ALLOWING THE EXTRAORDINARY TO UNFOLD.

Let me share another personal story. After working for years as a marketing director for the home builder I mentioned, I started feeling burnt out and trapped, with no clear path for advancement. Seeking a change, I actively pursued new job opportunities, but nothing aligned with my goals. Frustrated and exhausted from the job search, I embraced the saying, "Let go and let God."

Drawing upon my frequent use of manifestation techniques, I turned to my journal for guidance. Every day, I wrote, "I will leave my job by January 1, 2020," repeatedly filling the pages of my journal with this statement. This practice continued for months, spanning multiple journals. Despite lacking concrete plans or evidence, I persisted in writing this, gradually transforming any initial doubts into unwavering conviction.

While writing, I immersed myself in the emotions of joy and liberation that would accompany leaving my job. I visualized a life free from the daily grind, where I could spend quality time with my family and pursue new opportunities. This repetitive practice became a habit, and I faithfully wrote in my journal every evening, finding deep satisfaction in each entry. With each passing day, it became an ingrained belief in me. I didn't know how my manifestation would happen, but it would.

Then, five months later, in November, unexpected news arrived—the company announced its sale, and our last day of work would be December 31, 2019. While my colleagues experienced surprise and a range of emotions, I felt an overwhelming sense of achievement and calm. It was as if the Universe had aligned with my desires, and I had successfully manifested my intention. Adding to this synchronicity, I received severance pay, providing the financial security I had envisioned and allowing me to take an extended break.

But that's not the only example. In 2020, as the COVID-19 pandemic unfolded, I decided not to rush into finding a new job. Instead, I set the intention to attain enough financial stability to stay home with my family for the entire year. Expanding my practice beyond journaling, I incorporated nightly spoken affirmations into my routine. Crafting a list of resonant affirmations, I recorded them and listened to the recording every night before sleep.

True to my intention, money started flowing into my life from unexpected sources, steadily continuing throughout the year. This unexpected financial support enabled me to honor my intention and spend precious time with my loved ones.

As I neared the end of my year-long break, a profound sense of serenity and faith in the Universe's capacity to align my aspirations with opportunities enveloped me. I had witnessed the remarkable influence of repetition and unwavering belief in manifesting my deepest desires. It became crystal clear that the Universe was providing for me.

In an astonishing turn of events, just a week before Christmas and before I had even started a new job search, an old colleague from my previous job unexpectedly reached out to me. They extended an offer for a position at a different company. Fate seemed at work, as not only did I secure the job, but I also received a higher compensation package and promotion. Everything I had fervently wished for had miraculously materialized.

When coupled with unwavering belief, positive emotions, and purposeful actions, repetition strengthens the connection between our conscious and subconscious minds. It creates new neural pathways, solidifying positive beliefs and intentions within our subconscious.

We create a fertile ground for manifesting our desires through consistent exposure to empowering messages and affirmations. Our subconscious mind becomes a powerful ally, working in harmony with our conscious intentions to attract and bring forth the outcomes we seek.

It is important to remember that repetition is not the sole ingredient of this transformative alchemy. It works in harmony with other elements, nurturing our unwavering belief, fostering positive emotions, and inspiring purposeful actions aligned with our desires. Repetition perpetually reinforces our newfound beliefs and intentions, imbuing them with a profound sense of permanence within the depths of our subconscious mind. Together, these elements create a powerful synergy that paves the way for the manifestation of our dreams.

PART III

the path forward

"To thine own self be true."

WILLIAM SHAKESPEARE

LIVE IN ALIGNMENT WITH YOUR HIGHER SELF

IN HOMER'S EPIC poem, *The Odyssey*, the captivating story of Odysseus is an allegory for this quest for alignment with our higher self. As Odysseus endeavors to return home to Ithaca after the Trojan War, he encounters numerous trials and temptations that challenge his character and resilience. However, through his unwavering commitment to his true purpose and alignment with his higher self, he triumphs over these obstacles and emerges as a transformed individual.

One remarkable example that vividly illustrates Odysseus's alignment with his higher self is his encounter with the enchanting sirens. These mythical creatures wield an irresistible allure, employing enchanting songs to lure sailors to their doom. Yet, aware of this dangerous threat, Odysseus devises a strategic plan to navigate this treacherous obstacle while staying true to his deepest convictions.

To safeguard his crew, Odysseus instructs them to plug their ears with beeswax, rendering them deaf to the Sirens' captivating melodies. However, driven by a thirst for knowledge, Odysseus confronts the temptation head-on. He commands his crew to bind him tightly to the mast, ordering them not to release him, no matter his pleas.

As the vessel neared the Sirens' island, their alluring voices filled the air, reaching Odysseus. Though the song's power was profoundly tempting, Odysseus remained steadfast, bound as he had instructed. Odysseus emerged with his character strengthened through his unwavering commitment to his higher purpose and unyielding resistance to temptation. Not only did he safeguard his crew, but he also gained profound wisdom about the transformative power of self-control and staying true to one's deeper calling. Recognizing the Sirens' song would become irresistible, Odysseus had the foresight to restrain himself, allowing him to experience their vocals while ensuring his survival.

This episode exemplifies the importance of aligning with our higher self by honoring our values and purpose. Odysseus's unwavering commitment highlights the transformative power of remaining steadfast, even facing the most tempting distractions.

Through Odysseus's example, *The Odyssey* invites us to reflect on our lives and identify the temptations and distractions that hinder our alignment with our higher selves. It encourages us to remain steadfast in pursuing our true purpose, making choices that honor our values and propel us forward on our journey of self-discovery and self-actualization. This allegory powerfully resonates, serving as a timeless lesson on the profound rewards of self-mastery and integrity. By heeding Odysseus's example, we, too, can navigate life's trials with courage and purpose.

> YOU CAN CULTIVATE A DEEPER CONNECTION
> TO YOUR HIGHER SELF BY HONORING
> YOUR VALUES AND PURPOSE.

HOW TO ALIGN WITH YOUR HIGHER SELF

Aligning with your higher self is a profound and transformative endeavor. It demands a deep commitment to truly knowing yourself, honoring your core values, and summoning the courage to make choices that reflect your highest truth.

1. SELF-REFLECTION

Self-reflection is a crucial first step in living authentically. It involves regularly looking inward and examining your core values, beliefs, strengths, weaknesses, and life purpose. This reflective process allows you to understand what truly matters to you.

For example, you may discover that your core values include creativity. By reflecting on these values, you can assess how well your current lifestyle and choices align. You may realize that you've prioritized financial success over creative expression, which doesn't resonate with your authentic self. This insight can then inspire you to adjust, such as exploring more artistic hobbies or finding a job that allows you to integrate your values into your work.

2. IDENTIFY AND EMBRACE YOUR PASSIONS

Take the time to discover the activities, causes, or subjects that ignite a genuine sense of joy, purpose, and fulfillment within you. These things make you feel alive and energized, where you lose track of time because you're so immersed in the experience.

For instance, you may be deeply passionate about environmental conservation and protecting endangered species. This passion could manifest in volunteering for a local wildlife organization, participating in community clean-up efforts, or learning about sustainable living practices. These passion-fueled activities give you a sense of meaning and alignment with your higher self.

> FOLLOWING YOUR PASSIONS AND PURPOSE RAISES YOUR VIBRATION, ATTRACTS ABUNDANCE, AND ALLOWS YOU TO LIVE A PURPOSE-DRIVEN LIFE.

Conversely, if you find that much of your time is spent on tasks or hobbies that don't resonate with your true passions, it may be time to adjust. Incorporating more of your passions into daily life can provide a renewed sense of vitality, purpose, and self-actualization. Embracing and nurturing your passions is a powerful way to express your authentic self and live a fulfilling life.

3. SET BOUNDARIES

Learn to say no to things that don't align with your higher self.

This may mean declining certain obligations, relationships, or activities that drain your energy, compromise your values, or prevent you from engaging in more meaningful pursuits.

For example, you may find that you've been volunteering for an organization whose mission no longer resonates with you. Or perhaps you've been spending a lot of time with a friend group whose values and interests don't align with yours. By setting the boundary to decline these obligations or limit time with these relationships politely, you're honoring your higher self and creating space for more fulfilling experiences.

This can be challenging, as we often feel compelled to please others or maintain the status quo. However, setting healthy boundaries is an act of self-care and self-respect. It demonstrates that you value your own needs, priorities, and well-being. Over time, this practice can help you cultivate a lifestyle that aligns with your authentic values, passions, and purpose.

Saying no to things that don't serve your authentic self may feel uncomfortable initially, but it's a necessary step in owning and expressing your authentic nature. Setting these boundaries allows you to make room for the people, activities, and opportunities that help you thrive as your best, most genuine self.

4. LIVE COURAGEOUSLY

Living courageously involves taking risks and making decisions that honor your true self, even if they go against societal or peer pressures. This requires deep self-trust and the courage to forge your path rather than conforming to external expectations.

For instance, you may have dreamed of starting your own business, but societal norms and familial expectations have steered you towards a more traditional career path. Living courageously in this scenario would mean taking the leap and pursuing your entrepreneurial aspirations, even if it means going against the grain and facing potential criticism or uncertainty from loved ones.

This could manifest in quitting your stable corporate job to devote yourself full-time to launching your venture or taking a sabbatical to travel and gain clarity on your authentic calling. It might also involve speaking up and advocating for causes that are important to you despite the risk of backlash or ostracization from your social circles.

Living courageously is not about reckless or impulsive decision-making. Instead, it's about cultivating the inner strength to make choices that are true to your values and aspirations, regardless of what others may think. It's about bravery to step out of your comfort zone and embrace the unknown to honor your higher self.

This path may not always be easy, but it is a powerful way to live with integrity, self-empowerment, and fulfillment. When you dare to walk your unique journey, you inspire others and pave the way for a more authentic, meaningful life.

5. CULTIVATE SELF-ACCEPTANCE

Embrace all aspects of yourself, including the parts you may perceive as flaws or weaknesses. It's about practicing self-compassion and moving beyond harsh self-judgment or the constant pursuit of perfection.

For instance, you may have always been self-conscious about your shyness or introverted nature, viewing it as a limitation that holds you back. However, through self-acceptance, you can appreciate these qualities as unique strengths. You may recognize that your sensitivity allows you to connect deeply with others or that your introspective nature fuels your creativity and wisdom.

Self-acceptance is not about ignoring areas for growth or improvement but about approaching them with kindness and understanding. It's about acknowledging your humanity, its complexities and imperfections, and treating yourself with the same compassion you would extend to a dear friend or family member. This act of self-compassion is a way of valuing yourself.

This shift in mindset can have a profound impact on your life. When you fully embrace and accept yourself, you free up the energy you once spent on self-criticism. You become more confident in expressing yourself, taking risks, and pursuing your passions without fear of judgment. Self-acceptance also allows you to build deeper, more genuine connections with others, as you're no longer hiding behind a facade of perfection.

Cultivating self-acceptance is an ongoing journey, but it's a crucial foundation for living in alignment with your true self. By embracing all aspects of who you are, flaws and all, you learn to honor your unique identity. This journey requires courage, but it's this courage that empowers you to live authentically.

6. LISTEN TO YOUR INTUITION

Listening to your intuition is a vital step in living authentically. Your intuition, often described as your "gut feelings" or "inner voice," can guide you towards choices and decisions that align with your higher self.

For instance, you may consider a job opportunity that aligns with your skills and experience, but something within you feels uneasy about it. Perhaps the work environment doesn't resonate with your values, or the company's mission doesn't ignite a sense of purpose in you. You can decline the offer by tuning in to that intuitive nudge, even if it goes against societal or peer expectations of what you "should" do.

Conversely, you may feel a deep, almost inexplicable pull towards a particular path, even if it seems unconventional or risky. This could be the intuitive voice encouraging you to take a leap and start your own business, pursue a passion project, or relocate to a new city. Honoring these intuitive impulses allows your true self to emerge and guide you toward more meaningful and fulfilling experiences.

Developing the ability to listen to your intuition takes practice and self-awareness. It requires carving out time for introspection, quieting the external noise, and tuning into the subtle sensations and insights from within. Over time, as you learn to trust and act upon your intuitive guidance, you'll find that your choices and actions become more aligned with your authentic values, passions, and life purpose.

> BY HEEDING YOUR INTUITION'S WISDOM,
> YOU EMPOWER YOURSELF TO MAKE DECISIONS
> THAT HONOR YOUR TRUE SELF,
> EVEN AMID UNCERTAINTY OR SOCIETAL PRESSURES.

7. SURROUND YOURSELF WITH SUPPORTIVE PEOPLE

Surrounding yourself with supportive people is crucial in cultivating authenticity and living true to yourself. It involves seeking individuals who accept you as you are and who encourage you to embrace and express your authentic self.

For instance, you may have a close friend who has always celebrated your unique quirks and talents rather than trying to change or push you to conform to societal norms. This person may be the one who listens without judgment when you share your most profound dreams and fears and champions your unconventional career aspirations or creative pursuits.

On the other hand, you may have family members or colleagues who are quick to criticize or dismiss the aspects of yourself that make you different. These people may subtly (or not-so-subtly) pressure you to fit into a specific mold or make you feel ashamed for not living up to their expectations.

You create an environment that nourishes authenticity by consciously surrounding yourself with supportive, like-minded individuals. These people will uplift you, challenge you to grow, and provide a safe space to take risks and experiment with new ways of being.

Over time, the influence of these supportive relationships can profoundly impact your self-confidence, self-acceptance, and overall well-being. You'll feel empowered to embrace your true self, knowing you have a strong network of people who celebrate your unique gifts and support your authentic journey.

Surrounding yourself with supportive people is not about destroying relationships with those who may not fully understand you. It's about being intentional about the company you keep and prioritizing the connections that uplift and empower your authentic expression.

8. CONTINUOUS GROWTH AND EVOLUTION

Your authentic self is not a fixed or static entity but a fluid, ever-evolving expression of who you are. As you learn, experience, and transform, your true self may shift and grow in new directions.

For instance, you may have spent years pursuing a career path that once aligned with your passions and values. However, as you've gained new experiences and perspectives, you may find that your authentic self is now calling you towards a completely different vocation. Embracing this evolution may require you to have the courage to make a significant life change, even if it means leaving behind the familiarity and security of your previous path.

Similarly, your core beliefs, interests, and sense of identity may evolve. Perhaps you once strongly identified with a particular political ideology or spiritual tradition, but as you've grown and expanded your understanding, you now find yourself drawn to a different worldview. Honoring this evolution means being open to shedding old labels and embracing the nuances and complexities of your authentic self.

Continuous growth and evolution are not about constantly reinventing yourself or pursuing a state of perpetual change. Instead, they're about maintaining a posture of curiosity, self-reflection, and openness to transformation. They're about having the courage to let go of outdated aspects of yourself and the willingness to explore new facets of your authentic identity.

This journey of growth and evolution can be both exhilarating and challenging. There may be times when you feel lost or uncertain as you navigate uncharted territory. But by embracing this process with compassion and self-trust, you can ultimately deepen your connection to your higher self and live a life increasingly aligned with your evolving essence.

9. ALIGN YOUR ACTIONS WITH YOUR VALUES

Aligning your actions with your values is a critical step in living authentically. It ensures that your daily habits, decisions, and behaviors are congruent with your core values and beliefs, creating a life of greater integrity and wholeness.

For instance, you may have a profound passion for the natural world and all its wonders. This could manifest in regularly hiking or camping in nature, volunteering with a local conservation organization, or studying the intricacies of ecosystems. These passion-fueled outdoor pursuits give you a profound connection and alignment with your higher self. Leaning into these environmental passions can infuse your life with incredible wonder, stewardship, and spiritual renewal.

On the other hand, if you find a disconnect between your stated values and your actual behaviors, it may be a sign that you need to reevaluate your priorities or make some changes. Perhaps you value kindness and compassion, but you frequently are short-tempered or impatient with loved ones. In this case, you should explore the root causes of this incongruence and make a concerted effort to align your actions with your professed values.

Aligning your actions with your values can be challenging, as external pressures or personal habits may make it difficult.

However, you can create an authentic and fulfilling life by consistently checking in with yourself and making intentional choices that honor your core beliefs.

This alignment benefits you personally and has a ripple effect on those around you. When you live with integrity and authenticity, you inspire and empower others to do the same. Your congruent actions can be a powerful example and even influence positive change within your community and the world.

Aligning your actions with your values is a lifelong journey of self-discovery and conscious decision-making. But by staying true to what matters most, you can cultivate a deep sense of purpose, meaning, and authentic self-expression.

10. CULTIVATE MINDFULNESS AND PRESENCE

Cultivating mindfulness and presence is a powerful practice that can help you connect more deeply with your higher self. By staying grounded in the present moment, you can become less reactive to external distractions or societal pressures and instead tune into the wisdom and insights from within.

For instance, imagine you're facing a significant life decision, such as whether to accept a lucrative job offer in a city far from your loved ones. Amid the stress and uncertainty, it's easy to get caught up in worrying about the future or dwelling on the opinions of others. However, you create space to tap into your intuitive knowing by pausing, breathing, and bringing your attention to the here and now.

In this present-moment awareness, you may become more attuned to the subtle sensations and emotions within you. Perhaps you notice a tightness in your chest when contemplating the job offer or a sense of inner peace when you imagine staying close to your support system. These embodied cues can serve as guideposts, helping you discern what aligns with your authentic self rather than simply chasing external markers of success or approval.

Cultivating mindfulness and presence is an ongoing practice that involves regularly carving out time for quiet reflection, meditation, or simply being in nature. It's about learning to quiet the mind's chatter and turn your attention inward, allowing your true self to emerge and guide your choices and actions.

As you become more adept at staying grounded in the present moment, you may be less reactive to stressors, more attuned to your intuition, and better able to make decisions that honor your deepest values and longings. This presence-based approach can be a powerful antidote to the distractions and external pressures that quickly pull us away from our authentic selves.

By practicing mindfulness and presence, you create the conditions for your true self to thrive, empowering you to live a life of greater alignment, fulfillment, and self-actualization.

Embracing these principles of authentic living is not a one-time achievement but an ongoing, dynamic process. As you navigate the ebbs and flows of life, you'll continually be called to peel back the layers of conditioning, societal pressures, and self-limiting beliefs to uncover the radiant essence of who you truly are. By consistently tending to this inward journey of self-reflection and self-acceptance, you'll unlock the freedom to live a life that is deeply meaningful, richly soulful, and profoundly connected to your higher self. This path may not always be easy, but it is a journey worth taking—one that can transform your life and inspire and uplift those around you.

THE JOURNEY CONTINUES

"The journey of a thousand miles begins with a single step."

LAO TZU

THE JOURNEY CONTINUES

W E HAVE UNDERTAKEN a profound exploration—delving into the depths of the Universe and the interconnectedness of all things to understand how our thoughts, emotions, and beliefs shape our world. By immersing ourselves in the mysteries of our inner selves, we have uncovered the intricate interplay between these essential aspects of our being. As we reach this important milestone, let us pause to reflect on its profound impact and how it has shifted our perspective.

Cultivating deep self-love and self-worth lays the groundwork for change, creating an unshakable inner foundation supporting our highest aspirations. Self-acceptance and self-appreciation empower us to approach life with a spirit of abundance, recognizing our inherent value and worthiness of the blessings we wish to manifest.

Underlying our desires lies deeply rooted limiting beliefs and resistance that can hinder our efforts. We liberate ourselves from self-doubt and self-sabotage by bringing these subconscious patterns to the surface and addressing them with compassion. This inner exploration and transformation process clears the path for us to embrace new possibilities and align our actions with our highest aspirations.

Our thoughts unlock the full potential of manifestation. By consciously cultivating a positive mindset, we shift our focus from the limitations of the past to the boundless possibilities of the future. This mental reframe empowers us to see opportunities where we previously saw obstacles and approach challenges with an unwavering belief in our ability to overcome them. As we nurture empowering thoughts and beliefs, we lay the groundwork for a life brimming with infinite possibilities.

Gratitude is a powerful catalyst, aligning our energy with the vibration of abundance and appreciation. We open our hearts to receive even more by consistently expressing gratitude for our blessings. This gratitude practice elevates our emotional state and attracts more of what we desire, creating a positive feedback loop.

Effective manifestation requires clarity. By reflecting deeply on and articulating our desires, we focus on the creative power of the Universe, directing it toward our highest aspirations. This clarification process allows us to set clear, intentional goals that serve as our North Star, guiding our actions and decisions.

Intention is the driving force behind manifestation, as it infuses our desires with the power of focused attention and directed energy. By setting clear, specific, and aligned intentions, we create a magnetic field that draws our dreams into reality. This intentional focus shapes our thoughts and actions and imbues our journey with purpose and meaning.

The power of visualization lies in its ability to activate the neurological pathways associated with achieving our goals. By vividly imagining ourselves living out our desired outcomes, we condition our minds to believe in the reality of these possibilities. This practice of conscious visualization strengthens our connection to the manifestation process, making it more tangible and attainable.

Our inspired actions hold power to bridge intention and manifestation. Each step we take, and our choices can profoundly shape our world. Cognizant of this knowledge, we approach life with a heightened sense of responsibility and purpose. Unwavering in our commitment, we channel our intentional, inspired actions toward manifesting positive change, unlocking new realms of possibility.

By practicing forgiveness for ourselves and others, we release the weight of past hurts and resentments. This act of compassion and understanding allows us to move forward with a lighter heart, embracing the present moment and its infinite possibilities.

Transformation and manifestation are delicate dances between our efforts and the flow of the Universe. By cultivating an attitude of surrender and trust, we align ourselves with the natural rhythms of life, allowing the Universe to guide us toward our desired outcomes. This surrender is not a passive act but a conscious choice to let go of control and embrace the sacred mystery of the process.

Manifestation is not a one-time event but a continuous process of reinforcement and refinement. By consistently applying these techniques, we reinforce the neural pathways in our brain, solidifying our ability to create the life we desire. With each repetition, our abilities grow stronger, and we move closer to the fulfillment of our dreams, step by step, day by day.

Living in alignment with your higher self commands the same process as cultivating self-love and self-worth—a journey of self-discovery and self-acceptance. It involves uncovering your deepest values, passions, and life purpose and then consciously shaping your thoughts, beliefs, and actions to reflect this authentic essence. This solid foundation allows you to clear the path to new possibilities that align with your highest aspirations.

Embrace the fullness of your being and allow yourself to be in awe of your magnificence. Celebrate the transformative journey you have traversed and the growth you have undergone. Honor the courage to face your shadows and transmute them into gold.

As you continue to explore these principles, remember that you are both a perpetual student and a guiding teacher. Your blossoming has the power to inspire and uplift those around you. Together, we can create a cascading effect of positive change that uplifts our communities and the world.

BE THE ENERGY YOU WISH TO ATTRACT.

May your journey be abundant with profound transformations, awe-inspiring manifestations, and exponential growth. Embrace and celebrate the infinite possibilities that await you, and trust in the effortless unfolding of your desires, knowing that the Universe conspires in your favor. I wholeheartedly believe in you.

You are enough. ✧

ABOUT THE AUTHOR

T.L. Workman's lifelong passion for storytelling emerged in her early years as she diligently crafted books and shared them with her classmates. Her journey unfolded through roles as an entertainment editor, copywriter, marketing director, and consultant, creating impactful work reaching millions worldwide.

Driven by a profound sense of purpose, T.L.'s mission is to uplift and inspire others, empowering them to embrace the life they have always envisioned. Drawing upon her experiences and growth, she guides individuals on transformative paths to fulfillment, instilling hope and motivation to become their best selves.

T.L. resides with her family in Laguna Niguel, California, where she finds solace and joy in long walks along the beach, accompanied by the playful presence of her cherished Siberian Husky, Baymax.

ENDNOTES

I have carefully compiled a detailed list of references and citations for each chapter in this book. However, I acknowledge the possibility of inadvertently failing to credit specific sources appropriately or incorrectly attributing ideas to the wrong individuals.

If you notice any such issues, please email me at tl@tlworkman.com. This will allow me to address and rectify the problem promptly.

In addition to the reference notes in the text, I have also made available a comprehensive, updated list of endnotes and corrections on my website at tlworkman.com/endnotes. I encourage you to refer to this online resource containing complete and accurate attribution information.

Please feel free to bring any citation or referencing concerns to my attention. Ensuring proper credit is of the utmost importance to me, and I welcome your feedback to help improve the integrity of the citations in this work.

QUANTUM ENTANGLEMENT AND
THE LAW OF ATTRACTION

1. Sagan, C. (1980). *Cosmos*. Random House.
   "*The cosmos is within us. We are made of star stuff. We are a way for the Universe to know itself.*" [Quote]

2. Einstein, A. (1935). *Can Quantum-Mechanical Description of Physical Reality Be Considered Complete?*. Physical Review, 47(10), 777-780.

THE IMPACT OF THOUGHTS, EMOTIONS, AND BELIEFS

3. Buddha, G. (n.d.). *MN 19: Dvedhāvitakkasutta*. (Bhikkhu Bodhi, Trans.).
   "*Whatever one frequently thinks and ponders upon, that will become the inclination of his mind.*" [Quote]

SELF-LOVE AND SELF-WORTH

4. Rumi. (n.d.).
   "*You are not a drop in the ocean. You are the entire ocean in a drop.*" [Quote]

OVERCOME SUBCONSCIOUS
LIMITING BELIEFS AND RESISTANCE

5. Piper, W. (1930). *The Little Engine That Could*. Platt & Munk Publishers.

6. Wood, J. V., Elaine Perunovic, W. Q., & Lee, J. W. (2009). *Positive Self-Statements: Power for Some, Peril for Others*. Psychological Science, 20(7), 860-866.

7. Church, D., Hawk, C., Brooks, A. J., Toukolehto, O., Wren, M., Dinter, I., &

Stein, P. (2013). *Psychological Trauma Symptom Improvement in Veterans Using Emotional Freedom Techniques: A Randomized Controlled Trial.* The Journal of Nervous and Mental Disease, 201(2), 153-160.

8. Waite, L. W., & Holder, M. D. (2003). *Assessment of the Emotional Freedom Technique: An Alternative Treatment for Fear.* The Scientific Review of Mental Health Practice, 2(1), 20-26.

9. Wake, L., Gray, R., & Caswell, G. (2015). *The Clinical Effectiveness of Neurolinguistic Programming Approaches for the Treatment of Depression: A Systematic Review.* Psychology, 6(8), 1141-1158.

10. Carrington, P., & Colligan, R. (2011). *The Effectiveness of Neurolinguistic Programming Techniques in Reducing Public Speaking Anxiety.* International Journal of Advanced Counseling, 33(2), 96-110.

CULTIVATE A POSITIVE MINDSET

11. Churchill, W. (n.d.). *Quotes.* International Churchill Society. *"The pessimist sees difficulty in every opportunity. The optimist sees opportunity in every difficulty."* [Quote]

12. Seligman, M. E. P., Steen, T. A., Park, N., & Peterson, C. (2005). *Positive Psychology Progress: Empirical Validation of Interventions.* American Psychologist, 60(5), 410-421.

13. Boehm, J. K., & Kubzansky, L. D. (2012). *The Heart's Content: The Association Between Positive Psychological Well-Being and Cardiovascular Health.* Psychological Bulletin, 138(4), 655-691.

14. Moskowitz, J. T., Hult, J. R., Duncan, L. G., Cohn, M. A., Maurer, S., Bussolari, C., & Acree, M. (2017). *A Positive Affect Intervention for People Experiencing Health-Related Stress: Development and Non-Randomized Pilot Test.* Journal of Health Psychology, 22(8), 972-981.

15. Otake, K., Shimai, S., Tanaka-Matsumi, J., Otsui, K., & Fredrickson, B. L. (2006). *Happy People Become Happier Through Kindness: A Counting Kindnesses Intervention.* Journal of Happiness Studies, 7(3), 361-375.

PRACTICE GRATITUDE

16. Ward, W. A. (n.d.).
"Gratitude can transform common days into Thanksgivings, turn routine jobs into joy, and change ordinary opportunities into blessings." [Quote]

17. Kini, P., Wong, G. T., McInnis, S., Gabana, N. T., & Brown, J. W. (2016). *The Effects of Gratitude Expression on Neural Activity.* NeuroImage, 128, 1-10.

18. Zahn, R., Moll, J., Paiva, M., Garrido, G., Krueger, F., Huey, E. D., & Grafman, J. (2009). *The Neural Basis of Human Social Values: Evidence from Functional MRI.* Cerebral Cortex, 19(2), 276-283.

19. Ding, X., Tang, Y. Y., Cao, C., Deng, Y., Wang, Y., Xin, X., & Posner, M. I. (2015). *Short-Term Meditation Modulates Brain Activity of Insight Evoked with Solution Cue.* Social Cognitive and Affective Neuroscience, 10(1), 43-49.

CLARIFY YOUR DESIRES

20. Hill, N. (1937). *Think and Grow Rich.* Ralston Society.
"The starting point of all achievement is desire." [Quote]

SET CLEAR INTENTIONS

21. Edison, T. (1932). *Diary and Sundry Observations.* Harper & Brothers.

22. Gollwitzer, P. M., & Sheeran, P. (2006). *Implementation Intentions and Goal Achievement: A Meta-Analysis of Effects and Processes.* Advances in

Experimental Social Psychology, 38, 69-119.

VISUALIZE SUCCESS

23. Morgan, J.P. (n.d.).
"The first step towards getting somewhere is to decide that you are not going to stay where you are." [Quote]

24. Kosslyn, S. M., Ganis, G., & Thompson, W. L. (2001). *Neural Foundations of Imagery.* Nature Reviews Neuroscience, 2(9), 635-642.

25. Yue, G. (2013). *The Influence of Mental Imagery on Physical Performance.* Journal of Sport and Exercise Psychology, 35(4), 375-388.

TAKE INSPIRED ACTION

26. Picasso, P. (n.d.).
"Action is the foundational key to all success." [Quote]

27. Aarts, H., Custers, R., & Marien, H. (2008). *Preparing and Motivating Behavior Outside of Awareness.* Science, 319(5870), 1639-1639.

FORGIVE

28. Buddha, G. (n.d.).
"Holding onto anger is like grasping a hot coal with the intent of throwing it at someone else; you are the one who gets burned." [Quote]

29. Lama, Dalai. (1998). *The Art of Happiness.* Riverhead Books.
"If you want others to be happy, practice compassion. If you want to be happy, practice compassion." [Quote]

SURRENDER AND TRUST

30. Zen Proverb. (n.d.).
"Let go, or be dragged." [Quote].

REPETITION

31. Durant, W. (n.d.).
"We are what we repeatedly do. Excellence, therefore, is not an act, but a habit." [Quote].

32. Bruce Lee. (n.d.).
"I fear not the man who has practiced 10,000 kicks once, but I fear the man who has practiced one kick 10,000 times." [Quote].

LIVE IN ALIGNMENT WITH YOUR HIGHER SELF

33. Shakespeare, W. (1601). *Hamlet, Act 1, Scene 3.*
"To thine own self be true." [Quote].

34. The Journey Continues

35. Tzu, L. (c. 6th century BCE). *Tao Te Ching.*
"The journey of a thousand miles begins with a single step." [Quote].

INDEX

www.ingramcontent.com/pod-product-compliance
Lightning Source LLC
Chambersburg PA
CBHW021808130726

47987CB00010B/3060